This book can be tokenized. Scan the code to claim the digital token.

My Date with a Beatle

by JUDITH KRISTEN

Published by Imagine & Wonder
Irvington, New York 10533 USA
www.imagineandwonder.com

Scan this QR code with your phone camera
for more titles from Imagine and Wonder.

Your Guarantee of Quality: As publishers, we strive to produce every book to the
highest commercial standards. The printing and binding have been planned to
ensure a sturdy, attractive publication that should give years of enjoyment. If your
copy fails to meet our high standards, please inform us and we will gladly replace
it. admin@imagineandwonder.com

Cataloging-in-Publication information is available
from the Library of Congress.

Library of Congress Control Number: 2021944723
ISBN #9781637610107 (Hardcover)

First Edition

Printed in China by Hung Hing Off-set Printing Co. Ltd.

FSC
www.fsc.org

MIX

Paper from
responsible sources

FSC® C017606

Many Thanks To…

Frank Sinatra (not THAT Frank), Eric Cash, Steven Wilson, Simon Mills, Ruth McCartney, Dr. Angie McCartney, Patty, Shelly, Carole, Dottie, Frannie, and Mary G.

This book is respectfully dedicated to the memory of Mr. Elias Howe, who, in 1846, invented the sewing machine.

This book is dedicated to
John, Paul, George, and Ringo…and
Beatles fans everywhere!

FOREWORD

When I was asked to write the Foreword to Judith Kristen's book: "My Date with a Beatle" I was so pleased.

It has been my privilege and pleasure to have a friendship with Judith spanning many years, originally just online, then later face to face, after meeting up at some of Mark Lapidos' Fests for Beatles Fans, and over afternoon tea at my home in Playa del Rey on subsequent visits.

Her never ending optimism and enthusiasm for her favourite Fabs, and in particular, George, still has no sign of flagging, after all these years, from the time she played hooky from school to sneak off and watch their arrival at Kennedy Airport, to her subsequent pursuit of them at The Lafayette Motor Inn in Atlantic City, New Jersey, (—spoiler alert—where she actually DID meet her beloved George), and the never to be forgotten magic and mayhem that broke out when they first appeared on The Ed Sullivan Show, when we learned to share them with the world, instead of just our hometown of Liverpool. Between 1964 and 1965 Judith managed to wrangle tickets to 9 Beatle shows from the east coast all the way to Chicago. A true stalwart if ever there was one.

Judith has pursued her great interest by visiting Liverpool and Manchester several times, cementing friendship with many of the stalwarts of Beatledom, from Freda Kelly (Good Ol' Freda), to original Beatle drummer Pete Best to Bill Heckle, one of the owners of The Cavern Club in Liverpool.

In this whirlwind story, she captures the excitement and the planning of her foray into the Beatles world, and when you read this very entertaining book, you can put yourself in the mind of a youngster aiming for the stars and achieving what she had dreamed of doing for so long.

She continues to be a very active writer, and you can find some of her other works at ImagineandWonder.com.

So, let's wind the clock back to the summer of '64 and go along on a teenage Beatle fan's adventure!

Enjoy!

Dr. Angie McCartney
Los Angeles

AN INTRODUCTION

My dear friend of almost 60 years, Patricia Mehaffey-Secor is really the one to thank for this book.

Back in the very beginnings of Beatlemania, Patty and I were both working after school down in the kitchen of Frankford Hospital, in Philadelphia. You know, the usual teenage thing to earn some of your own money.

Pat and I became fast friends for many reasons: we enjoyed each other's sense of humor and mischief, we loved to dance, to communicate about everything under the sun, we loved ice cream, jukeboxes, The Holmesburg Bakery, and we loved our Rock and Roll roots that started way back when we were 7 or 8 years old in the early 1950s. What a cool way to grow up!

Then came The Beatles.

It was life-altering.

And, while Patty was a bit more sensible about her Beatlemania, she championed me onward in my quest to meet George Harrison and enjoyed my hair-brained schemes and we would laugh about them on a regular basis.

I was quite hush about many of my "Beatley" escapades, especially early on, because I would have been grounded until I was fifty. Not that I was above tying sheets together and heading out my bedroom window, but still...my parents didn't need to know e-v-e-r-y-t-h-i-n-g.

Time marched on and Pat suggested that I should write about 1964 and the magic of that entire year before it got distorted by time.

You know, what it was really like to be a rabid Beatles fan back in the day. The times when no one knew what LP was coming out next, when we had no idea a film called 'HELP' would be another Beatles movie... or where they would tour the following summer.

I said, "I guess writing about it would be cool," and I gave it some thought. But within a few short years, I found myself living in Germany as an Army wife and I had four small children, so there was no time for writing things like that, just reflections and quite a few smiles as I played their records for my kids, or the joy I found singing them to sleep with songs like, "Goodnight," "This Boy," or "Penny Lane."

Fast forward several decades: I was almost 60, when I finally said to myself, "Self, you gotta write this book."

And so, I did. That took a lot of searching for diaries from olden days but coupled with the fact I'd been telling the story for decades by then, I could practically recite it in my sleep, and the writing was a breeze—and so much fun!

As for my 'unknowing' parents? I eventually told my mother when I was 35. I figured a 20-year gap from the time of the incidents would be a safe harbor by then.

All Mom said to me was, "I'm not surprised."

Take that as you will.

Well, before I start telling the story, before the story starts to tell itself, I'm going to end this here with a smile on my face, knowing what is yet to come for you and knowing that I'm going to sit down and enjoy reading it again right along with you.

Let's have some fun!
Peace and Love to you all…
And Beatles 4 ever!
…And ever.

~Judy

PROLOGUE

1963 sucked.

My father was hospitalized twice for alcoholism, my favorite aunt and uncle died within weeks of each other, my best friend was killed in a car crash, and then, on November 22nd of that same year, John Kennedy was assassinated.

I was ready to jump out my bedroom window, but it was on the first floor…so, why bother? Toying with the idea was drama enough.

And America?
Musically?
Puh-leeze.

America was nowhere.

Long gone were chart toppers: Buddy Holly, Ritchie Valens, and The Big Bopper. A plane crash in '59 saw to that. Chuck Berry all but vanished after he got in trouble with the law for violating The Mann Act, and, when hot rocker Jerry Lee Lewis married his thirteen-year-old cousin, well…his heyday and paydays were over.

As for Elvis? To me, he was never the same after he got out of the Army.

It just broke my heart to see him in all those bad 'B' movies. I mean, from a smokin' hot song like, *That's Alright Mama* to… *Clambake?!*

I wanted to scream.

The closest America came to anything new at all was The California Sound. It was making a few waves on the East Coast (no pun intended) but truly, for a Philly girl, all that surfin' shit was totally lost on me.

And those songs about a "Woody?" That always made me laugh. It might have meant a cool car to the folks out in sunny southern California, but it was a totally different ball game in Philadelphia. Again, no pun intended.

Then came December 10, 1963… and my life was changed forever.

I remember walking into the living room just as Walter Cronkite was about to end The Evening News. My father was a huge Cronkite fan, another one of his addictions, and he was glued to the television. I walked by and he waved me off with the shake of his hand.

"What the hell is this?" he grumbled.

I turned toward the set and saw four shaggy-haired young men from a place called Liverpool, England, singing to what appeared to be hundreds of frenzied fans.

I walked closer to the old Motorola.

"They're cute!" I practically swooned.

"Jungle music," Dad grunted.

"Jungle music? Dad, they're English!"

"English Schminglish! It's a disgrace!"

"What's so disgraceful? It's just music."

Ignoring my remark my father continued his rant. "And look at that hair! Can't they afford a decent barber? Where are their parents? Can't they…"

Dad's words were completely lost on me. All I could do was watch every move they made and listen to every note they sang until the single most beautiful moment on American television news was over.

I was captivated and consumed…to say the least.

Much to my parents' continual dismay my heart often beat to a different drummer…but now things were even more different, the drummer had a name—Ringo.

But the man who immediately and totally captured my fifteen-year-old heart was the lead guitarist.

His name was George Harrison.

And the band who played that jungle music?

The Beatles.

CHAPTER ONE

"I'LL GET IT!" I said running out of the living room and heading straight toward the wall phone in the kitchen. It was my friend, Shelly.

"Jude! Did you see Cronkite just now?!"

"YES! My God! Talk about timing! I was walkin' into the living room the second it came on!"

"I like the drummer." Shell marked her territory fast.

"I like the lead guitar player!"

"So what are they called again? The Bubbles?"

"Shell, they're The Beatles."

"Oh, yeah. And what was the song they were just singing?"

"It Won't Be Long."

…And it wasn't.

America was *instantly* bitten by the love bug…or love bugs as it were.

And, in just eight weeks and three days, 1,416 hours later, (but who's counting?) they would grace our shores with their presence.

I couldn't wait!

The time and place were set for their first official television appearance in the United States: The Ed Sullivan Show—Sunday, February 9th, 1964.

Again, I couldn't wait!

Savvy businessmen totally understood this cash cow, known as "The British Invasion", and did everything they possibly could to rake in some BIG bucks: Beatle games, Beatle wigs, Beatle lunch-boxes, Beatle pencils, Beatle key chains, (deeeeep breath) Beatle buttons, Beatle bracelets, Beatle glasses, Beatle coffee mugs... Beatles everything! And none of the hype was wasted on yours truly.

I worked at a local hospital after school and on weekends, so I had some of my own spending money since long gone were the days when a fifty cent a week allowance was enough. I now had $28.00 a week to spend on whatever I chose.

My first Beatles purchase was a *Meet The Beatles* album from Bond Record Store on Frankford Avenue—$1.99. I was first in line the day it went on sale.

"Your father was just in here yesterday, Judy," the manager said as he put my money into the cash register. "He purchased *Madame Butterfly*, Van Cliburn's *Rachmanino⊠ Concerto Number 2*, and another copy of *West Side Story*."

"What? No Beatles?" I smiled.

"Not that I recall." He smiled back.

I clutched the new album to my chest.

"Well, apparently I'm the only one in the family with any real taste in music."

Again, he smiled at me.

From the Philadelphia Inquirer, circa 1964: The Beatles giving their famous bow to adoring fans.

CHAPTER TWO

Before February even thought of rolling around, my bedroom was plastered with pictures of The Beatles from one end of it to the other—ceiling included.

I heard my mother whining to my Aunt Dorothy about it.

"I picked out that Wisteria pattern for Judy myself. It was the most beautiful wallpaper at Silverman's. Now her room looks like some crazy Beatnik record shop!"

"Martha," my aunt said softly, "she's a good student and if this is all she ever gets into, consider yourself lucky."

"I guess," Mom sighed.

"It's just some silly band. She'll get over it. No harm done. I mean it's not like she's cutting school or anything."

CHAPTER THREE

Friday, February 7, 1964
7:25 AM
Wakeling Street

"Shelly?" I whispered into the phone. "Are you goin' or not?"
"I can't."
"Why?"
"My mom'll find out!"
"So what? So will mine! But they'll find out AFTER we see them land at Kennedy!"
"I can't do it."
"Fine then. I'll go without you."
"No, don't! Wait! What time will we get back?"
"They land around 1:30. We'll follow them in a cab to their hotel, hang around there for a while, and then take the bus back home. We oughta be back right after dinner, just like a regular school/workday."
"No...I can't. I'm too scared."

"Some fan you are. I swear to God, if I see Ringo I'll never even mention your name to him, I swear it!"

"Alright, alright. I'll go."

"Really? Cool!"

"No...I...I can't. I'll get killed. I can't cut school!"

CHAPTER FOUR

Friday, February 7, 1964
1:16 PM
Kennedy Airport

"I was squished in-between a big redhead and a girl who looked like one of The Ronettes. There was also a guy right behind me with a short Beatle haircut who kept pushing himself up against me—if you know what I mean.

I was an in-your-face kinda kid, even then, and he wasn't about to get away with it. I yelled at the top of my lungs, "THIS CREEPY GUY BEHIND ME IS PUSHING HIS PENIS UP AGAINST ME!!!!"

Within twenty seconds two cops came and carried 'Ron Jeremy' away.

Where to? I had no idea.

But…adios, creepo.

"That was weird," the redhead announced.

"The creeps are everywhere." I looked skyward and then added, "Except on Pan Am Flight 101, that is."

She sighed and then proudly displayed her *I Love Paul* button. "He's sooooo dreamy."

I nodded. "I like George."

The Ronette turned toward me. "Well, I love George and I've got the right look. You know, he had a huge crush on Estelle Bennett from The Ronettes. I've got the same eyes, the same hair color. Why don't you like John? He likes blondes."

"John's married! I can't like a married man!"

"Well, you're wastin' your time on George." Then she laughed at me, "You look like a poster girl for the Oktoberfest. He likes exotic women. He'd never give you a second glance."

"You know what," I said, staring right into her heavily made-up cat eyes, "why don't you just go f…"

She never heard me finish my sentence because at that precise moment, The Beatles plane came into view and I heard an uproar I never imagined possible…and my own voice was part of it.

"OH, MY GOD!!!!!!!!!!!!

OH…MY…GOD!!!!!!!!!!!!!

GEORGE!!!!!!!!!!!!!!!

GEORGE!!!!!!!!!!!!!!!!!!!!!!!!"

Then everything went black.

CHAPTER FIVE

When I came to, a wiry cop who looked like a young Groucho Marx was carting me off somewhere. I managed to walk alongside of him, although my legs still felt a bit wobbly.

"Where we goin'?"

"We're goin' where ya won't get into no trouble."

"Are you sendin' me back to Philly?"

"Just follow me, Blondie!"

A few minutes later I shuffled my way into a room that was buzzing with activity: reporters, cops, newspaper folks, more cops...

"Sidd-down ovah there." He pointed.

I turned to my left.

Five girls stared back at me—all wearing Beatle buttons: two that read, I Love Ringo, one I Love Paul, one generic, I Love The Beatles and then a red, white, and blue, Yeah, Yeah, Yeah, button.

"Go on...siddown!" he barked at me.

"Okay...Okaaaay."

As I took my place on the already overloaded bench, someone else was ordered to sit down in the only available spot—right next to me.

It was the creepy guy that I squealed on.

"You know, that wasn't very cool," he bitched, "I coulda got arrested."

"Well, remember that the next time you decide to play your, 'Willy and the hand-jive' bullshit, okay?"

"How old are you?" he said eyeing me up.

"Old enough to know you're an asshole."

That ended that conversation.

The other girls on the bench looked terrified and never said a word. I could tell they were envisioning calls to their parents, no allowance for a year, and definitely no watching The Ed Sullivan Show that Sunday night.

None of that stuff worried me in the least.

Not a chance.

All I knew was that right then and there I had an opportunity for adventure, and I was gonna take it.

I scanned the room carefully until I finally realized exactly where we were. I watched all the Press, TV crews, and photographers go straight through a door not ten feet away from me.

"Hurry up, Eddie…they're startin'."

Startin'?

As the door closed, and the cop guarding it walked away, I sat there creating a game plan.

Soon I heard commotion, some laughter, and I could see that through the gap between the floor and the bottom of the door that there were lots of flashbulbs going off!

My God…they're in there!

I got up from the bench and headed straight for the door.

"Just where do you think you're goin'?!" Groucho said to me.

"Oh…I…uh…I gotta walk around a bit. You know… cramps."

He rolled his eyes and then turned his back to me.

I quickly made my move and leaned up against the door, flash-bulb lights sparkling on my loafers.

Suddenly I heard a man with a New York accent ask, "Listen, I got a question. Are you going to get a haircut at all while you're here?"

And then I heard George's beautiful Liverpudlian voice answer back to roars of laughter, "I had one yesterday."

That's all I needed.

My hand was on the doorknob.

I looked around to see if any cops were watching me.

And then…I cracked the door open.

There they were! Right in front of four microphones and a huge Pan American Airlines sign.

THE BEATLES!

My heart raced like a jackrabbit.

I was just about to make a fast un-thought out run for the podium when the heavy hand of doom and gloom suddenly rested itself upon my shoulder.

"Cramps?! Cramps?!!" Groucho yelled at me, "Whaddya think I am, stupid?"

"Is this a pop quiz?" I smiled.

"Siddown ovah there, wise-ass!"

Reluctantly, I sat back down on the bench and tried my best to tune into what was happening just one door and ten feet away from me. All I could hear was laughter, some loud questions, obviously from the rear of the room near the door, and of course, those flashbulbs never stopped.

A police sergeant walked over to all of us with a grim look on his face. He then took out a small pad and pencil. He looked at the 'I Love Ringo' girl who was farthest away from me and barked, "STAND UP! What's your name and where are you from?"

"Sir," she said, with a voice that crackled in-between tears, "My name is…is Sharon Anne Miller and…and I'm from Asbury Park and I live at…"

"And YOU?" he continued the same question right down the line and the answers were as follows:

"Lorraine Pisano, Brooklyn…"

"Mallory McDonald, Tenafly…"

"Shelly Fredman, Hoboken…"

"Diane Levitz, Yonkers…"

Then he turned toward the only guy on the bench. "And *you*, young man?"

"Allen Johnson, Long Beach Island."

"Johnson," I smirked, "how appropriate."

Both officers then turned to me. "And how about you, resident troublemaker?"

"My name is Judy…um…Judy Martin." (I used my grand-mother's maiden name) "I'm from…New Haven."

"I thought you said you were from Philly?"

"Well, I am! I mean, I was…we…we just moved to New Haven."

The two officers walked away from all of us, appeared to be discussing our fate, and then made their announcement.

"Well, now that we have your information," then the sergeant turned to look at me and continued, "well, *maybe* we have all of your information…here's our advice: Get outta New York and STAY OUT!"

Without as much as a minute's notice we were each assigned a police officer who was told to put us into a cab that would take us to the nearest connecting train, subway, or bus, heading 'The Troublemakers' back home.

"This one's from New Haven!" my cop yelled at the cabbie and then handed him some kind of voucher. "Sarge said take Blondie straight to her front door!"

CHAPTER SIX

I turned up my transistor radio as far as it would go, pushed the earpiece into my ear tightly, and then tuned in WABC New York. According to 'Cousin Brucie', The Beatles would be staying at The Plaza Hotel—on the twelfth floor.

"Hey," I said to the cabbie, "How about we make a deal with that voucher?"

"Whaddya tawkin' about?"

"You don't *hafta* drive me to New Haven." "Says who?"

"Says me. Look, you seem like a pretty smart guy. How 'bout I just fill in the voucher so that it *says* New Haven, so then you get *paid* for New Haven and…."

"And?"

"And, all ya gotta do is just drive me into the City." "Like where?"

"I need you to drive me to the twelfth floor of The Plaza Hotel. I mean, I need you to drive me to The Plaza Hotel."

"And that's it?"

"Yep…that's it."

CHAPTER SEVEN

Twenty-five minutes later I was standing on FAO Schwartz's sidewalk, directly across from The Plaza. There were already at least two thousand girls outside the hotel, so it was nearly impossible for Mr. New Haven to drop me off right outside the building. But that was okay with me. My goal was within view and that's all that mattered.

I stared upward, counted twelve floors, and sighed.

A cop on a horse waved a crowd of us across the street, so I followed orders—for once.

A few twists and turns and orders from some more cops, and I found myself in Central Park right across from the hotel.

Again, I stared upward, counted twelve floors, and sighed.

At that very moment four shaggy heads appeared in one of those twelfth-floor windows.

I screamed.

I waved.

And I screamed again.

I mean it, even though it was twelve floors up from where I stood, I coulda sworn George saw me and he waved back to me!

"HE SAW ME!" I shrieked, "GEORGE SAW ME!!!"

"Are you kidding?! He was waving at me! Get over yourself!"

I turned to my immediate left and there she was again…the Ronette.

"I'm going to The Sullivan Show on Sunday," she bragged. "How about I wave to you so you can see me on TV."

"Well, *I'm* gettin' into the hotel this afternoon. How about I wave to *you* from there!"

"You're so full of crap," she said snapping her gum at me.

"Oh, yeah? You just wait and see. Tenacity's my middle name, sister!"

CHAPTER EIGHT

It took a lot of intestinal fortitude, athletic prowess, and some deep elbow nudges into the sides of a few dozen fellow teenagers, but I finally made my way to the front of The Plaza Hotel.

"Hey!" I called out to a nearby police officer, "I *have* to get in there!"

"WHAT?!"

I waved him toward me. "I SAID I HAVE TO GET IN THERE!!!" The look on my face was a dramatic combination of sincerity, angst, and passion.

The officer made a few fast moves in-between four horse cops and then, there he was standing right in front of me.

"What's the matter?"

"I *said*..."

"I heard what you said."

"Well then?"

"Oh," he smiled, "You think I'm gonna escort you into the building? Who you gonna visit? Aunt Alice on the seventh floor?"

"How did you know my Aunt is in there? I mean, not my Aunt Alice, but my Aunt Mary."

He shook his head. "Sweetheart, every one of these girls has a relative in that hotel today."

"But they're lying!"

"And you're not?!" he laughed.

"Listen, my mom's sister is in there. I'm kinda their liaison, see…they've been on bad terms over the years, and…and… I kinda…well, I was the…the catalyst that brought them back together."

He looked me straight in the eye trying to make me back down from my story, but I was on a mission and my future marriage to George Harrison was at stake, so I stayed the course. "She didn't know The Beatles were here when she made that reservation! You gotta know that!"

"I see…"

My confidence was building, and I continued, "Anyway, I'm an American girl, all the way. I like The Beach Boys. Now if *they* were in here…" I chuckled, "well, you'd be gettin' some trouble from me too! You know, like all these other girls are with The Beatles."

"Your Aunt Mary, huh?"

"Yep," I smiled. "Aunt Mary."

"What's her last name?"

"McGillicutty." I figured if I said a name, any name, real fast, it would be more convincing.

"Mary McGillicutty is your aunt?"

"Why not? Don't I look Irish enough for you, Officer…" Oh, brother…his name tag read, *O'Brien*.

"No, you don't. You look like a poster girl for the Oktoberfest."

I gave him an offhanded look. "You know, that's the second time I heard that today."

Damn that Saint Pauli Girl.

He smiled. "So you're Irish, huh?"

"As Irish as Paddy's Pig," I smiled back. "Listen, I can prove it, just take me in there to the reservation desk and if my Aunt Mary isn't registered there, then just bring me back out here, and boot me back home."

He stared at me for a moment or two. "Well, I don't know, I..."

"Awww, come on. One fellow Irishman to another?!"

"Ah, alright. Come on. But no funny business."

"Are you kidding? This is serious stuff!"

I crouched down and was on the other side of the cop barrier in about two seconds.

Officer O'Brien never left my side and we entered the beautiful hotel: huge Persian carpets, gigantic vases, The Palm Court... it was magnificent. I had to think fast because the reservation desk was now in full view.

"Wait a sec, I have to tie my shoe!"

"Go ahead," he said as he kept on walking.

Thank God he didn't notice I was wearing loafers.

The minute O'Brien separated himself from me, I saw that big brass elevator door open and a man with a luggage rack quickly enter it.

I moved faster than I ever had in my entire life and soon found myself standing right next to the Bellboy.

"Where to, Miss?" he smiled.

"The twelfth floor, please."

NUMBER NINE...

The heavily scrolled door closed and I was totally confident that I was on my way to meeting George, his asking me out on a date, and then, falling madly in love with me.

I turned to the Bellboy and said, "Where are you going?"

"Same place you are."

Then I carefully eyed his fancy baggage cart. "You know, The Bubbles are up on that floor."

"You mean The Beatles?"

"Oh, yeah," I said innocently.

That said, we arrived at the third floor, the doors opened but no one was there.

"So," I continued, "Have you seen them?"

"Sure. I was just up there. This is the last of their luggage."

I leaned in toward the suit carriers imagining George's grey Chesterfield jacket, his black topcoat, or his black turtleneck sweater inside them. Then I saw a small suitcase with a Pan Am label attached to it, and right under that was a weathered address label that read:

G. Harrison
25 Upton Green
Speke
Liverpool, England.

I think I was drooling.

Then the fifth floor door opened, and an elderly gentleman entered. He smiled at us, pushed the sixth-floor button and then off we went, ascending once again.

"Can I just pop in and say hi before I go to my Aunt Mary's room?"

"In The Beatles room?"

"Sure, why not? A nice American greeting. They'll like me more than Murray the K, I can tell you that much."

He laughed. "Yeah, he's a bit obnoxious alright."

Soon the sixth-floor bell rang and the nice old man left me and my favorite Bellboy alone once again.

"Well?"

"Well, I might get into trouble. I really can't invite you and…"

"Hey, I'll play it like I never even saw you before, I'll just walk in behind you, that's all."

He shrugged his shoulders at me and smiled. "Okay. No harm done, I guess."

NUMBER NINE...

The elevator door opened to even more chaos than there was outside the building: photographers, newspaper people, local police, disk jockeys, and—Oh, Dear God, I almost couldn't believe my own two eyes!—Beatles Management! Not three feet away from me were the Beatles right hand men and friends: Neil Aspinall, Brian Somerville, Mal Evans, and Derek Taylor. I recognized them from my teen magazines. I gave all four of them a slight smile and kept right on moving behind George's luggage. I was practically glued to it.

Maybe no one bothered me because they thought it was MY luggage! At any rate, when the two of us walked passed a barrier of sorts that protected all of the Beatles suites, I knew I was home free!

Their manager, Brian Epstein, nodded a polite hello and I nodded back.

BRIAN!!! Oh, my God! BRIAN!!! I'm almost there! Oh, dear God!!!! Three feet!...Two feet!...

My bellboy pal politely tapped on the door, some old man, roughly age forty, answered it. I craned my neck around the luggage rack and I could see John Lennon laughing into a telephone and Paul playing with a small transistor radio that looked just like the one I had.

Oh, my God! I'm in! I am sooooo in!!!

Just then I saw George from the back and I couldn't help myself; I called out to him, "GEORGE!!!"

As he turned toward the sound of my voice and I was blessed enough to see that gorgeous profile of his, I felt someone grab me by the back of my coat.

It was a cop.

"Hey!" I said wriggling myself out of his grip, "I'm *going* to see my Aunt…"

"Who? Your Aunt George?!"

"Yes, my Aunt George! Well, her real name is Georgette but…"

"And George just happens to be your nickname for her, right?"

"Exactly. Now, please…I have to get going." I was desperately trying to keep a certain mature decorum about myself.

"You're stayin' right where you are, sister."

"Really, officer, I have to leave, I'm late! I'm here to visit my Aunt!" Just as those words left my mouth another policeman stood right next to me talking into a special kind of radio.

"Yeah, she's a blonde…about five feet eight inches tall…yeah, black stadium jacket…"

I watched as the two policemen talked to each other, but I couldn't hear a word they said for all the commotion going on.

Then, they both turned back toward me.

"Time to get you back downstairs where you belong."

"I *belong* up here!"

"Nice try, kid."

Before I knew it, I was back inside that beautiful elevator with two linebacker-sized cops right beside me.

Not one of them said a word.

"This is unfair, ya know."

No answer.

"I'm underage. This could get nasty."

Still no answer.

"I have my rights as a citizen!"

Absolutely no response.

"Don't you cops have *anything* to say?!"

Just then the lobby bell rang, the door opened, and finally there was a policeman who had a few words for me. "Well, hello, Miss McGillicutty," smiled Officer O'Brien.

NUMBER NINE...

"I'll take it from here," he said to the two linebackers.

"You sure?"

"Yeah. She's done her damage for the day. Haven't you, McGillicutty?"

I sneered at him. "I wanna talk to my lawyers!"

"Oh, do you? And just what are their names?"

"Dunn and Overwith." I smiled.

He sighed and shook his head. "Look, here's the plan, Mrs. Harrison. You get yourself into a cab and back to Port Authority, and go home." He looked at me in a strange manner and then asked, "And just where is home?"

"Ummm, I'm from..."

He put his hand out in front of me to put the lid on my end of the conversation. "Don't even tell me. You got enough money to get there?" he asked as we walked toward the doorman.

"Yep."

I really did have money, but I'm not so sure he believed me. ...I wonder why.

"Look, here's ten bucks. Take a cab to the station and make it home safely. Your life of crime has just come to a grinding halt."

I took the ten dollars and put it inside my jacket pocket. "Thanks. But...but can I at least exit the building with a little style?"

He shook his head at me. "What's that supposed to mean?"

"Well, can you escort me to the taxi without having it look like you're taking me to Leavenworth?"

"You promise you'll go right home?"

"I promise."

He let out a heavy sigh, "I don't know how much faith I have in that statement, but...let's go!"

A doorman in a beautiful regal-looking coat with shiny buttons held the hotel door open for me as if I was The Queen of England. "Thank you for visiting The Plaza, Miss. Please come back again soon." He smiled.

I turned to Officer O'Brien, "See, *he* was happy I was at The Plaza! 'Come back again *soon*,' he said. Didja hear that?"

Again O'Brien shook his head.

Within seconds the two of us were standing at the top of the steps to The Plaza entrance. I pulled my "I Love George" button out of my pocket, pinned it quickly to my jacket and then waved and blew kisses to the largest crowd of girls I had ever seen in my life.

"Did you get to the twelfth floor?!" one girl screamed. "DID YOU SEE THEM?!"

"YES!" I hollered back. "I saw John and Paul...and George!!!"

"NO RINGO?!" someone yelled.

"Hey," I called out, "Three outta four ain't bad!"

"Officer? Did she *really* see them?!" another voice belted out.

"Yes, according to my fellow officers, she did."

I turned toward that voice and there she was again…my old pal, the Ronette.

I gave her a big toothy smile.

She gave me the finger.

…I love New York.

CHAPTER TEN

I caught the 4:58 bus at Port Authority. The way I figured it, I should be walking up Wakeling Street at 7:20 PM, just like any other school/workday during the week.

For the entire bus ride, I relaxed, and changed the channel on my transistor radio in search of another Beatles song the instant one had ended.

Life was good.

What a great day!

Shelly would be green with envy, of course, but...that's what she gets!

Before I went home, I had to stop off at my friend Pat's house. See, I borrowed Patty's black stadium jacket for the day. We were the same size, so she wore my camel coat with the raccoon collar to school and I got her black stadium jacket. We always traded clothes, so the switching coat routine came as no surprise to her mom. It was just another girly teenage thing.

The actual idea behind it was that if by any strange reason I would be photographed, and my parents saw what they swore was me, I could always say, "Hey! You saw me when I left this morning! I only have this one winter coat. It's camel colored with a fur collar, not a black stadium jacket!"

Who said my life of crime was over?

I walked into the house through the breakfast room door and looked at the clock to my left: 7:21.

Perfect.

"I'm home!" I called out.

"We're in here," my mother answered.

I hung my coat up in the dining room closet and then as I was walking by the television and my parents, Mom said, "How was your day today?"

"My day? Ummm…well, I cut school, took the bus up to New York to see The Beatles all by myself, got in trouble with half a dozen cops, and then…"

"Oh, Judy, for goodness sake…"

My father laughed, "You crazy kid. What an imagination! No, seriously, how was your day, Sweetheart?"

"Actually, Dad…it was interesting and quite enjoyable."

"Well, that's nice to hear, Honey. Very nice to hear."

Sometimes parents are totally clueless.

…Thank God.

CHAPTER ELEVEN

Shelly called me at 8:00 on the dot. I didn't want to risk having my parents hear anything, so I told the "No-Show" I'd drop by her place the next day and tell her all about "B-Day." February 8th was the only Saturday I had off from work that month, so I knew I wanted to enjoy myself, and what a better way to do it than by talking to Shelly about my day with The Beatles.

"You have GOT to be kidding?! You SAW their press conference?! Hey, I saw part of it on TV!"

"Well," I said taking a bite of my burger, "I saw part of it in person!"

"You dog, and you actually got into the hotel? My God, you've got balls."

"As brass as the doorman's buttons."

"Are they as cute in person?"

"What? My brass balls?"

She rolled her eyes at me. "The Beatles, for chrissake."

"Shell," I said, seeing a visual of them before me, "they're gorgeous!" Then I added, "You know, their first concert's at the

Washington Coliseum on the 11th. There's tickets left. I heard it on the radio."

"You're not thinkin' about goin', are you?"

"You're not thinkin' about NOT goin', are you?!"

"It's in D.C.! We can't get tickets in Philly."

"Yes, we can," I said, "At Glassman's."

"Glassman's?"

"That ticket agency at 13th and Locust. They always have last minute seats for everything! They cost a little more, but so what? This is The Beatles!"

"Oh, I dunno."

"Look, Shelly, the Carnegie Hall dates are all sold out: two shows on the 12th, 7:30 and 9:30. Gone! So we're screwed if we don't get to D.C."

"Geez, Jude, I…"

"You know YOU are the hemmin' and hawin'-ist person I've ever known. I don't even know how we stay friends!"

"Alright, look…how would we get there?"

"Train."

"How are they gettin' there?"

"Train."

"How much will it all cost?"

"I guess around twenty-five bucks."

"I only have forty-nine left."

"Shell…I only have forty-six left 'til payday, but, if my mathematical calculations are correct, that *still* means we have more than enough to see them at their first ever American concert!" I took the last bite of my hamburger, and a sip of my Coke. "So, I'll tell ya like I told ya last time. I'm goin' whether you go or not."

"Nah…" she said tossing her napkin into the trashcan, "it's too risky."

"Have it your way, kiddo." I got up from the soda fountain counter, left a tip, and then headed toward the door.

"Wait!" Shelly said, hurrying to catch up with me. "How cute did you say Ringo was?"

"He's not cute. He's gorgeous!"

"Alright. I'm goin'."

"You're not gonna bail on me at the last minute are you?"

"No way. I'm goin'!"

CHAPTER TWELVE

As we left Tree's Deli on Frankford Avenue, Shelly and I decided that the next day, a forever holy day in the annals of Beatles Fans everywhere, that we would each watch The Ed Sullivan Show in our own homes, you know, to have our own personal one on one moment with the boys.

I also dropped a dime into the phone booth on the corner and called Glassman's.

"Hello, could you please tell me if you have any tickets left for The Beatles concert in Washington on Tuesday night?"

"I have four." The man answered in a somber tone. "You have to buy two or four."

"I want two! How much are they?"

"Fifteen dollars. Each."

"Fifteen?! I heard they were four dollars!"

"Well, if you got them in D.C. last week, they would have been four dollars, but here, in Philadelphia, three days before the concert, they're fifteen."

"How late are you open tonight?"

"Until 6:00."

"We'll take them! My name is Judy. I'll be there in about a half an hour! Thank you!" I hung up the phone and turned toward Shelly whose mouth was now hanging wide open.

"You just bought t-t-t-tickets?"

"You know I did!"

"But I didn't even ask if I could go!"

"Look, are you goin' downtown with me or not? You got fifteen bucks on you?"

"Yeah, but…"

"Then let's get goin'."

"But…"

"No more buts. Let's get goin'!"

CHAPTER THIRTEEN

At 5:46 PM, according to Glassman's wall clock, Shelly and I were official ticket holders to The Beatles First American Concert.

"And they're pink! Your favorite color!" I smiled.

I read my ticket out loud in almost prayer-like fashion: "Washington, Coliseum. 3rd and M Streets, N.E. Washington, D.C. Tuesday evening, February 11th, 1964. 8:00 PM. Section 2, Row B, Seat 6. The Beatles!"

Shelly was looking at me as if I had just read a warrant for her arrest. "Even if I can go, we'll be back after midnight, and we have school on Wednesday."

"No, we don't. It's Lincoln's Birthday!"

"Oh, yeah."

"Listen, I'll tell my mom I'm stayin' overnight at your house and you tell your Mom you're stayin' over at mine! When we get back, my Mom will be sound asleep, Dad's outta town. So we'll just slip on in."

"Oh, God…this is worse than if I went to New York with you."

"Look, I got fifteen bucks on me I can give you right now for that ticket."

"No, I…"

"Someone'll want it, Shelly. I won't lose any money over this."

"I *really* wanna go, but…I just can't."

"Listen, you watch them tomorrow night on Ed Sullivan and if you still don't wanna go, I'll buy the ticket from you. Deal?"

"Deal."

CHAPTER FOURTEEN

Sunday, February 9th, was like molasses in January, or February, well…you know what I mean.

I don't remember a day passing by so slowly in all of my fifteen years on Planet Earth.

Every hour was another countdown for me: ten hours and they're on…nine hours and they're on…

Torture!

Torture!

Torture!

A few gal pals called: Pat, my old friend Doris G., and of course, Shelly, but we were all so excited about The Sullivan Show we really weren't very good conversation for one another.

I cleaned my room, tacked up a few more George pictures on my mirror—there was no space left on the walls or ceiling—and I took our darling mutt, Buttons, out for a walk.

Still it was only 2:00 PM.

I decided to iron some of my school clothes, then I helped Mom set the table for dinner, all the while listening to Beatles music and updates through the earpiece in my faithful transistor radio.

By the time dinner rolled around I was too jumpy to eat. Mom was a great cook and a Sunday pork roast with all the fixin's was my favorite, but I just pushed the food around on my plate.

"Aren't you feeling well?" Mom asked.

"I've got an acute case of Beatle-itis," I said. "It'll be over by 9:00 PM."

My mother shook her head at me.

By the time I helped Mom wash the dishes and I took Buttons out for another walk, it was 7:00 PM. One hour to go! Thank heaven! I ran upstairs and brought my favorite, framed picture of George back down with me. I turned the dial on the old Motorola back and forth: ABC, NBC, CBS, ABC, NBC, CBS—anything to distract me and make the time go by faster.

FINALLY…it was 8:00!

And about Mr. Sullivan? I used to think Ed liked teenagers, you know, he introduced America to Elvis and Jerry Lee Lewis, Buddy Holly…. I remember seeing all those guys on his show. They were great!

But when THEEE show came on, Ed made us wait almost twenty-five minutes before we got to see The Beatles!

But, oh, God…unfair as it seemed initially, it was so worth the wait.

The time finally came and, as I sat just as close to the TV screen as was humanly possible, just me and seventy-three million other Americans heard these exact words:

"Now yesterday and today our theater's been jammed with newspapermen and hundreds of photographers from all over the nation, and these veterans agreed with me that the city never has seen the excitement stirred by these youngsters from Liverpool, who call themselves The Beatles. Now tonight, you're gonna twice

be entertained by them. Right now, and again in the second half of our show.

"Ladies and gentlemen… The BEATLES! Let's bring them on!"

As if I wasn't enough in love with these guys, The Ed Sullivan Show sealed it up for me.

WOW!

WOW!

WOW!

and

WOW!!!!!

When they first stepped out on the stage they opened with Paul McCartney singing, *All My Loving* and I was immediately in Liverpudlian heaven.

Funny but I never saw the need to scream at a television set before that in my entire life!

Oh, well.

By the time the show was over, Paul had also crooned, *Till There Was You*, John sang, *She Loves You*, Paul sang, *I Saw Her Standing There*, and John ended the night with, *I Want To Hold Your Hand*.

George and Ringo didn't get to sing, but they were so cute! Ringo must love to play the drums, he just sat up there and smiled and shook his shaggy head the whole time. He was totally adorable!

And Mr. Harrison? Well, George had this beautiful, crooked smile, and when he sang harmony, his lip curled up a bit and… and he was absolutely gorgeous!

Oh, what a wonderful feeling to be fifteen and in love with an unavailable, twenty-year-old musician from a foreign country.

Judy's favorite picture of George Harrison, which sat in a frame on her nightstand throughout the Sixties. She added the following love notes: "Isn't he beautiful?" and "The Love of my life! XOXO 2/14 now to 4ever."

CHAPTER FIFTEEN

Within seconds of the Beatles taking their final bow of the evening, the telephone rang.

"I'm goin' on Tuesday night and I don't care if my parents disown me! RINGO!!!! Is he like the cutest thing ever?! How close are our seats to the stage? What time are we leaving and..."

Needless to say Shelly's former hemming and hawing had bitten the dust and she was finally starting to see things my way.

...About time.

"Shell," I said, "If you didn't flip over these guys, I woulda sent an ambulance over to check your pulse!"

"Oh, my God!!! And we're gonna see them in less than forty-eight hours!"

"In the flesh!"

"I'm so excited I feel like I could run from here to California and back!"

"Well, you'd be runnin' behind me," I laughed.

"You know," she sighed, "*if* I can even get to sleep tonight, I hope I dream about Ringo."

I smiled. "Less than forty-eight hours, Shelly."

"Life is good, isn't it, Jude?"

"It sure is."

CHAPTER SIXTEEN

Thank God Monday was a full school day *and* I had to work at the hospital. It sure took my mind off of Tuesday…well, almost.

The entire school was buzzing about The Beatles.

The girls were crazy about them, some of the jerky guys made fun of them, but the boys who really liked The Beatles remained cool about it. Then there were a few who were growing their hair long—"just because." …Hah!

Even in class there was no escaping The Beatles.

Shelly was in Mr. Fromberg's second period history program with me and every time he mentioned England, we'd look at each other and smile.

In-between third and fourth period I went to my locker to add a few more George Harrison photos to the collection.

Just then, Dr. Dickie walked by—the sternest, toughest, English teacher that Frankford High School had ever known.

"Well, Judith, I certainly hope this obsession of yours doesn't harm your grades."

"No, Ma'am. In fact, they've given me renewed interest in Shakespeare and Dickens and anything about Great Britain!"

"We'll see about that." She grunted and walked away.

Unexpectedly, my locker-mate Franny showed up. "What'd she want?"

"Who, the Princess of Darkness?"

Fran chuckled. "Yeah."

"She just wanted to make sure that my grades weren't going to go down the tube now that I was addicted to The Beatles."

"Oh, geez."

"Yeah, well…"

"Ya think she ever had anything goin' on in her life other than diagramming sentences when she was our age?"

I shrugged my shoulders. "I dunno. Maybe she liked playing fetch with the dinosaurs."

Franny laughed. "Hey, mind if I add a photo to the locker?"

"Well, since I'm the sophomore and you're the freshman, you have to have my approval, ya know. Let's see it."

Fran handed me a beautiful 8" × 10" color photo of The Beatles when they played at The London Palladium.

"Franny," I smiled, "put that one right here, dead center!"

CHAPTER SEVENTEEN

My tenth period class was over at 3:45, and, as always, I ran out of the building and down to Frankford Hospital to get ready to start my workday.

My friend, Pat, worked there with me, so it really made the evenings fly. We always had such fun. Patty was a really great kid. She liked The Beatles too, but she had a boyfriend named Fred, so, her before and after hours were pretty much spoken for.

And, Fred had a motorcycle.

At least that was pretty cool.

"Did ya get to see Ed Sullivan last night?" I asked as soon as I saw her.

"I saw the first part, but then Fred came over and…"

"Don't say another word. You're gonna break my heart."

"Hey, I like them, too! You know I'm crazy about Paul, but…"

"But?"

"It's just a band, Jude."

"So, you don't think you've gotta snowball's chance in hell of ever meeting Paul?"

She smiled at me. "I think the snowball's got a better chance."

"Patty, Patty, Patty," I said shaking my head. "Shame on you *and* your snowball."

Again, she smiled at me.

"You know, you can say what you want, Patricia, but my money's on The Beatles."

"What are you talkin' about?"

"I mean, they'll be around a lot longer than good old Fred will."

She laughed at me.

"I'm not kiddin' Pat. When I'm sixty-four they're still gonna be playin' The Beatles on the radio."

"Well, if they are, I'll tell you what, I'll be the first to admit I was wrong."

"You're a good sport, Mehaffey. I'll hold you to it. Let's see… when I'm sixty-four is…"

"It'll be in 2012."

"Wow! Wonder what I'll be like in 2012?"

It took Patty no time at all to give me an answer. "You'll be different," she laughed. "Old and different."

CHAPTER EIGHTEEN

February 11, 1964
7:55 AM
A late school day

I woke up and realized that in exactly twelve and a half hours I would be right in the middle of my very first 'live' Beatles concert and my heart did a flip. I turned toward my nightstand and smiled at George's picture.

Just then, my mother called up the steps, "I'm going to the A&P! Do you want anything?"

"One George Harrison to go, please."

"What did you say?"

I walked to the top of the stairs. "Nothin', Mom. I'm fine."

No sooner was my mother out of the house and my record player was spinning my *Meet The Beatles* album for what was probably the 500th time.

I quickly ran downstairs to call Shelly before I left for school.

"Hello," I smiled into the telephone, "Is this the future Mrs. Ringo Starr?"

"Yes, I believe it is. And is this the future Mrs. George Harrison?"

"It is if I have anything to do with it!" I laughed.

"Geez, Jude…" Shelly sighed.

"What?"

"We actually get to see them tonight!"

"Yup. We'll be breathing in Beatle air!" I was giddy at the thought of it.

"You're not bringing any jellybeans, are you?"

"Huh?"

"You know to go along with all of that Beatle air?"

"Why?" I asked.

"Because you know the boys love them and girls always throw them on stage!"

"Forget the jellybeans. If I throw anything on stage, it'll be me!"

She laughed. "Okay, so what time are we gonna meet?"

"Be at the Tioga El stop at 4:30."

"Okay."

"And don't bring a pocketbook. Just put your ticket, school ID, and some cash in a small purse and stuff it in your bra."

"Stuff it in my bra?"

"Hey, you got nothin' else to fill that thing."

"Very funny."

"It's just safer that way…that's what I meant."

"Okay, okay, will do."

"Yo, Shell, what are you gonna wear tonight?"

"My plaid skirt, my white shirt with the Peter Pan collar, and my burgundy crew neck. What are you wearin'?"

"Well, I'm feeling equally colorful. I'm wearing my black skirt, my black turtleneck, black leotards and my short black boots."

"That's colorful old you, alright. Okay, see you at school, Mrs. Harrison."

"And, I'll also see you at the El stop at 4:30. Be there or be square, Shelly."

"Jude, I wouldn't miss it for the world!"

CHAPTER NINETEEN

Shelly bitched the whole way down on the train about: how cold it was, how the snow would make her hair frizz, and that if her mother knew she was a hundred and twenty-five miles away in D.C. instead of four miles away at my house, she'd be dead meat and.... "Always the negative with you." I rolled my eyes at her.

"It is not!"

"Yes it is! Too much money for the tickets, too cold, too snowy, frizzy hair, your mom'll kill you…"

She turned her back to me in the seat. "And *you're* not concerned?" she huffed.

"Are you nuts?! These very tracks outside this window are the same tracks taking *our* boys to the *same* place we're gonna be tonight. There's not a negative thought in my head!"

She turned back to look at me.

"I…I know it'll be worth it, but…"

"No buts, Shell. It's worth it already and we're not even there!"

CHAPTER TWENTY

The commotion inside The Washington Coliseum made Kennedy Airport look like child's play.

The plus in all the ruckus was that Shelly and I had great seats. We'd only be about fifteen feet from our idols. How lucky could we get?

We could see Ringo's Ludwig drum set the minute we sat down. I thought Shelly would pass out! And me? I wasted no time at all as I sat there looking around trying to figure out where they would enter the auditorium, and how I could get at them when they did.

"Why aren't you talking?" Shelly asked me.

"I'm plotting."

"I was afraid of that."

"Hey, if they come up *this* way," I said, pointing right to the end of our row, "I could run up behind them and..."

"And what? Be the fifth Beatle? I thought that was Murray the K's job."

I gave her a big smile. "Not anymore."

Just as I was about to holler, "Let's get this show on the road!" the show was ready to start.

Truthfully, neither of us paid any attention to the opening acts. I mean, that wasn't why we bought our tickets! Was it?

Shelly was still fretting over what would happen if her mother found out, while I was busy scheming a way to make a safe run for the stage. Everything was out in the open, so that should make it easy. It was 360 degrees worth of Beatles once they got up there.

What could possibly go wrong?

CHAPTER TWENTY-ONE

It happened so fast I hardly knew what hit me. All of a sudden there was total mayhem. I heard a wave of screams, looked to my left, and there they were walking toward the stage—one beautiful Beatle after the other. Shelly was already up on her seat screaming for Ringo.

…In her nice safe seat.

Me? The instant I saw George, I made a run for it! No cop was gonna stop me this time!

I plowed my way through at least three-dozen girls, five or six policemen, flying stuffed animals, and forty pounds of jelly-beans. And, just as I was within arm's reach of my favorite Beatle, my skirt got caught on something sharp, and as I pulled to free myself, my skirt ripped straight up the back. The momentum immediately made me fall forward, and just as I was about to crash land onto George's boots, a cop grabbed me, I lost my right shoe, and once again, my perfect plan was foiled by a man in a blue uniform.

"GET BACK IN YOUR SEAT!" he screamed at me.

"BUT I LOST MY SHOE!" I hollered back.

"YOU'RE GONNA LOSE YOUR CONCERT PRIVILEGE IF YOU DON'T GET BACK WHERE YOU BELONG!"

There was no point in discussing the matter any further, and I certainly didn't want to get kicked out of The Coliseum, so I hobbled back to our Row B, now being pushed and pulled by the same girls I had pushed and pulled a few moments earlier.

Eventually I made it back to my seat…and to Shelly. In less than four and a half minutes I felt like I had aged fifty years.

Shelly stopped screaming just long enough to look at me. "What the hell happened to you?!"

CHAPTER TWENTY-TWO

O nce the show started I didn't care what I looked like, or where my shoe was. The Beatles were onstage, I was fifteen feet away from them, and I was ready to Rock and Roll with the four men I loved most in the whole wide world.

I watched as the stage filled with other people besides The Beatles. One guy took the mike and introduced Ringo. (Just ONE Beatle?!) I didn't understand what that was all about, but it made lotsa Ringo fans happy. ...Especially Shelly.

The boys tuned their guitars, fiddled with the speakers and re-situated Ringo's drums more than once.

Shelly yelled in my ear, "Who do you think will sing first?"

"George!" I answered.

"Nah, it'll be John, because he's the leader."

"NO! It'll be George because someone up there likes me!"

Shelly laughed. "Lotsa luck."

No sooner had those words left my mouth when Gorgeous George Harrison stood at the mike to my left and started to sing, *Roll Over Beethoven.*

I nudged Shelly in her side. "See? I toldja someone up there likes me!"

John...
Paul...
Ringo...and...
George...
George...
George...

I was mesmerized.

I never had so much fun in my entire life and I knew the Beatles were having fun too! Paul was bouncy and smiled all night long. John always looked like he was having fun, so did Ringo. And George? Well...he did that cute little dance with his feet every now and then, he smiled his crooked smile, and I was more in love with him when the night was over than I was when it started.

I didn't know how that was possible, but I was.

CHAPTER TWENTY-THREE

Roll Over Beethoven
From Me to You
I Saw Her Standing There
This Boy
All My Loving
I Wanna Be Your Man
Please Please Me
Till There Was You
She Loves You
I Want to Hold Your Hand
Twist and Shout
Long Tall Sally

That was the set list. Thirty-two and a half minutes of pure musical heaven.

When it was over...I was exhausted. One shoe short, one skirt ripped up to my ass, and totally exhausted. "Oh, my God, Jude!

I'll see this night in my head for the rest of my life!" "That makes two of us, kiddo."

"And Paul even sang a Little Richard song!"

"I know, *Long Tall Sally*! My favorite!"

Shelly and I were HUGE Little Richard fans. What a night!

After the boys left the stage, the cops tried their best to get all of us out of the arena in as orderly a fashion as possible.

Eight thousand formerly frenzied fans were now still buzzing, but far more mellow and easy to move along their way.

Well, except for me that is.

"Move it, Blondie!" another boy in blue instructed me.

"Officer, I lost my shoe! I can't go out in freezing, snowy weather with one shoe! We live in Philadelphia. We gotta take the train. I *have* to find my shoe!"

The man had absolutely no sympathy for me whatsoever, but fortunately a nearby female police officer did.

Shelly and I looked around for almost fifteen minutes, the officer helped us too, but we all came up empty.

"What am I gonna do?" I sighed.

The policewoman thought for a moment or two and then said, "Follow me, ladies."

Shelly and I ended up in what I guess was some sort of maintenance office, you know filled with a few guys who were going to do the cleanup after the building emptied out.

"This kid lost her shoe out there."

The guys looked at each other, one spoke up and said, "This ain't no Lost and Found or a Buster Brown Shoe Store, Officer."

The five men laughed, and I could feel my face turn red.

"Look," she continued, "Don't you have any snowshoes back there, something, anything that she can wear just to get back home. These kids are from Philly!"

"I'll take anything you have," I said. "I'll mail them back here, I promise."

The oldest of the five men got up and said, "Alright, wait a minute. Lemme look."

In less time than it took me to lose my shoe, Jake, according to his white nametag, came back with a pair of boots in his hand.

BIG, bright yellow, floppy rubber boots—size fourteen to cover my size eight and a half feet.

Shelly immediately burst into a fit of laughter.

"I'll take them!" I said reaching for the glow-in-the-dark Paul Bunyans.

I took my left shoe off, stuck it in my coat pocket and then put the boots on my feet. Shelly was still laughing.

"Honey," the officer smiled, "Are you sure you can walk in those things?"

"Sure," I smiled back. "No problem. I'll just have to remember not to lift my feet, so I don't fall out of them. Thank you!"

Shelly continued to laugh as I shuffled my way out of the maintenance room, and as I shuffled myself up the steps, and then again as I shuffled myself outside and into a waiting cab and back to the train station.

"Laugh as much as you want, Lady, but I was only two inches away from George Harrison when I lost that shoe, and if…"

"Yeah," she laughed again, "and IF he could only see you now!"

CHAPTER TWENTY-FOUR

The train ride back to Philadelphia was uneventful. That is if you don't count the fourteen times I walked out of those gigantic galoshes.

But, the minute we walked into my house—just after 2:00 AM—all was well. Thank God. Dad was gone, Mom was asleep, and those huge, ugly yellow boots were off my feet.

"Are you hungry?" I asked Shelly as I looked into the fridge.

"Whatcha got?"

I started to pull out some stuff to make roast beef sandwiches.

"How's this?"

"Great!"

"You want mayo?"

"Okay."

"Tomatoes and onions?"

"Sounds good to me."

"On toast?"

"Please."

"Hot chocolate?"

"I'd love some!"

With an armful of meat, bread, veggies, and condiments, I turned toward Shelly.

"Wonder what they're having now?"

"The Beatles?"

"No, The Bubbles. Of COURSE, The Beatles!"

"Probably nothin'," she said, taking some of the stuff out of my hands. "Well, maybe they're havin' a scotch and Coke and a cigarette."

I sighed. "See…that's artsy stuff. A scotch and Coke and a cigarette. We need to be more artsy."

"Don't get any funny ideas." She shook her head at me.

"Who, me?"

"Yes, you."

"Shell…Mom's got cigarettes up in the cabinet in the bathroom and…"

I stopped myself mid-sentence as my eyes once again fell upon the site of those size fourteen yellow-as-the-noonday-sun galoshes.

Shelly was right.

No more funny ideas.

I already had enough misadventure for one lifetime.

…or so I thought.

CHAPTER TWENTY-FIVE

The week couldn't go by fast enough for me. Sunday, February 16th, was another Ed Sullivan show and our boys would be on it!

This time from Miami.

Now they were 1,182.3 miles away staying at a place called The Deauville Hotel.

I called there almost a dozen times, person to person: I was John's Aunt Mimi, Paul's Aunt Gin, Ringo's girlfriend, Maureen, and George's sister, Louise. …you get the idea.

No one at The Deauville was buying it even though by then I had perfected quite the British accent.

So much for faking out a few savvy hotel operators. Oh, well, it was still worth the try.

And, since I only had $19.57 to my name, a plane or train ride to The Sunshine State was out of the question. So, I stayed home, played my *Meet The Beatles* album for the gazillionth time, went to school, walked to work, and decided to be normal for a while.

Whatever that was.

Finally, the five days from the D.C. Coliseum passed and it was again a Beatles Sunday.

Their second appearance on Ed Sullivan was performed in the Napoleon Ballroom at The Deauville. I couldn't wait to read the press reports and my jaw nearly dropped off when I read that the top-billed act on the show, was not The Beatles, but an American singer and dancer named Mitzi Gaynor.

Mitzi Gaynor?!

What the...??? MITZI GAYNOR?!!!

Well, Miss Mitzi might have had the top billing, but the real stars of the show were my loves from Liverpool.

Ed did the same setup as he did the week before when they performed in New York—they sang in the first half of the show, and then again, right after 8:30.

The set consisted of *She Loves You, This Boy, All My Loving, I Saw Her Standing There, From Me To You, Till There Was You,* and *I Want To Hold Your Hand.*

When John sang *This Boy* I actually had tears running down my face.

Their harmonies were beautiful, and the boys looked happy and rested. Miami apparently agreed with them. Ringo's face seemed a bit sunburned though. I guess he had just a little bit too much of that good old Florida sunshine.

And George?

I have to mention George.

He didn't get to sing a solo, but I could hear his voice in those harmonies, and it was perfect.

At the end of the show, I called Shelly and we laughed and giggled and were just so happy, so elated to see them perform three times in the very same week!

This is what heaven feels like.

I just know it.

CHAPTER TWENTY-SIX

February 22, 1964
Doomsday

Fifteen days in February from Beatles beginning to Beatles end raced on by. But those two weeks and one day gave me some of the best and most adventurous times of my life.

With a heavy heart I watched our television set as The Beatles left Miami, flew to New York, and then jetted back home to England.

I didn't even consider going back to Kennedy to see them off—not that anyone in security would have missed me. So, I worked that Doomsday Saturday and moped through most of it.

At least Pat was comforting. She said, "Jude, don't feel sad. They're comin' back in August! I heard it on the radio this morning. Think of what you can plot with all of *that* time on your hands!" She smiled and then walked away.

I heard her words again in my head...*Think of what you can plot with all of that time on your hands!*

All of a sudden, I felt so much better.

The next Sullivan performance was the following day, Sunday, February 23rd, 1964. Technically, this was their first performance, because The Beatles recorded this show on February 9th, 1964, before their historical first 'live' appearance. I didn't feel ripped off or anything, it was still wonderful to see them, taped or not.

In fact, it made it seem as if they were still in America with us.

I sang along with every song, I laughed, I cried…the full tilt teenage drama routine.

The Beatles played three songs: *Twist and Shout, Please Please Me*, and *I Want To Hold Your Hand* and, as always, I was glued to the television set. Well, me and seventy-three million other people that is.

At the end of the show Mr. Sullivan thanked The Beatles for "being four of the nicest youngsters."

Well of course they were, they were The Beatles!!!!

CHAPTER TWENTY-SEVEN

February 25, 1964
George Harrison's 21st Birthday

Earlier in the month I had written to Her Majesty, Queen Elizabeth, asking if the day could be declared a National Holiday in Great Britain.

No word back yet.

CHAPTER TWENTY-EIGHT

The thought of The Beatles back home in England was a heartbreaker for most American teens, but, we consoled ourselves with their music, the fact that they were making a movie to be released in July, and, as my dear friend Pat reminded me every so often, they'd be back again in August!

In-between all that hopefulness, there was a special closed-circuit showing of the Washington Coliseum concert, airing on March 14th.

Pat had to work that day, my other friend, Doris, had a very strict father who thought The Beatles were Satan's children, so she never even mentioned the 'B' word at home, so, once again it was a drag to ask Shelly, but I did.

"What is it again?"

"It's a closed-circuit kinda thingy."

"So what's that?"

"I guess it's just like a private showing of the concert we saw in D.C."

"But we already saw it." She shrugged her shoulders at me.

"So what are you saying?"

"I'm saying, we already saw it!"

"So why not see them again? Maybe we'll even see us! We were close enough to the stage!"

"Where's it playing?"

"The Logan Theatre."

"Where's that?"

"In Logan, Shelly."

"Oh, yeah."

"Well, how much does it cost?"

"Two bucks."

"When is it?"

"Saturday, March 14th. Look, you wanna go or not?!"

"I'm...well, I'm not sure."

"That does it!"

"That does what?"

"Enough already! I'm goin' and if you can make up your mind and you wanna see me *and* The Beatles, just look for the Oktoberfest's poster girl when you get inside the theatre."

I left the house on Saturday, March 14th right around noon and who did I see walking up Wakeling Street to meet me?

Yup.

Shelly.

"Well, look who it is! Shelly the Gemini."

"Shelly the what?"

I pulled out the 'Tiger Beat' teen magazine I brought with me to read on the bus and explained it to her.

"See, it's about a certain sign in the heavens when you were born. Like a certain month and day makes you a certain sign."

"Sign?"

"I was born on April 3rd, so I'm an Aries. You were born on June 5th, so that makes you a Gemini."

"Judy, what in God's name are you talking about?"

I stopped walking and opened the magazine. "Look, John is a Libra, George is a Pisces, Ringo is a Cancer…"

"Ringo has cancer?! Oh, my God!"

"Shell, it's a *symbol*. He's Cancer the Crab. And Paul is Gemini the Twins, like you!"

All of a sudden, her Ringo/Cancer drama flew out the window. "I'm like Paul McCartney?! What does it say?"

I flipped to the 'Paul' page and started to read: "The people who are born under the sign of Gemini are commonly known for their dual personalities and facility to rapidly change moods and opinions," I laughed, "that's you alright." I continued, "The twin sides of their nature are continually pulling them in conflicting directions. Their brains are clever and bright but those lesser-evolved 'Twins' will lack 'continuity of purpose.'"

"So you think I lack a continuity of purpose?"

"What kind of stupid question is that? I've known you for ten years and you've always lacked continuity of purpose. You know, your famous hemmin' and hawin' act."

"Oh, so that means Paul does too, right?"

"Shell…it said the lesser-evolved. I don't think Mr. McCartney falls into that category."

She grabbed the magazine away from me, "Lesser-evolved, my ass. Lemme see that thing!"

She quickly flipped to the page where the description of my sign, Aries the Ram was. "This crap's written by snake-oil salesmen. It's nothin' like us at all. Listen…here's you. It says: Aries is the first of the zodiac signs. Aries tend to venture out into the world and leave impressions on others. They are exciting, vibrant, and talkative. Aries tend to live adventurous and 'on the edge' lives. They are 'Go-Getters.' Once a bee is in the bonnet of an Aries, there is nothing that will stop them from reaching their goal. Tenacity is their middle name." Shelly grunted and handed the magazine back to me. "Yeah," she sighed. "That's nothin' like you at all."

When we arrived at the Logan Theatre the crowd of girls was as frenzied as if a live concert was about to take place. And there were men outside, hucksters of sorts, selling Beatles buttons, pennants, and even Beatles wigs!

I bought three more George buttons. Now my coat was sporting six of them—my latest fashion statement for 1964.

When we got our tickets, I looked at mine and said, "What the hell is this?" Then I noticed a HUGE poster directly in front of me that said the same thing as my ticket! "Shelly, LOOK!" I read the poster out loud as she stood beside me.

"In Full Concert—A Great New Show!
Closed-Circuit Big Screen
THE BEATLES
Direct from their 1st American Concert
at the
Washington, D.C. Coliseum.

And, on the same show
The Beach Boys!
America's Surfing Singing Sensations!

And…Leslie Gore!
She's the nation's No. 1 Teenage
Singing Sweetheart!"

We looked at each other.

"The Beach Boys?" Shelly questioned. "Leslie Gore?!" I practically gagged. "Just shoot me now. What the…?"

Shelly re-read the poster in disbelief. "They weren't even at The Coliseum concert! What happened to Tommy Roe and The Chiffons and…"

I shook my head. "This is crazy."

Shelly was totally puzzled. "Why would anyone put The Beach Boys and Leslie Gore on a film with The Beatles if they weren't even there at the concert?"

I sighed. "The popularity factor. To sell more tickets, I guess."

She shook her head, "Geez, aren't The Beatles enough?"

"Well, they are for us and that's all that matters."

"We're the last of the red-hot loyalists. Aren't we, Jude?"

"You can say that again."

"We're the last of the red-hot…"

"I know, Shell, I know."

CHAPTER TWENTY-NINE

Once we sat in the theatre and the closed-circuit show began and I had to sit through The Beach Boys singing: *Surfer Girl* and *Surfin' USA* and God knows what else. I was about to cry into my half a dozen George Harrison buttons.

The Beach Boys were all wearing those old-fashioned hairdos from the 1950s. In fact, one of the guys looked like in another year he'd be needing to sport one of those Beatles wigs the hucksters were selling outside the theater. The 'Boys' all wore striped shirts and plain beige pants, and there was no passion on stage like when the Beatles performed. No smiles between the boys! No movement! No joy! Three words could describe them: Blah, blah, and blah. Come on, guys…this is Philly! We need some ACTION! And *Surfin' USA?* Where? In the Delaware River with waves that reach four inches high?

Surf's up?

…I don't think so.

I'm sure The Beach Boys were very nice fellas, but…puh-leeze.

Shelly sensed my unhappiness and nudged me. "Hey, the best is yet to come…your gal, Leslie Gore!"

I gave her a blank look. "Remind me to hit you over the head when we leave here."

No sooner had Shelly mentioned good old Leslie, and there she was on screen with her cute, cherubic face and that highly hair-sprayed 'flip' hairdo snapping her fingers and singing, *Sunshine, Lollipops, and Rainbows.*

And as if that wasn't bad enough the entire audience was snapping, dancing, and singing along—word for word—with 'The Nation's Number One Singing Sweetheart.'

Those kids weren't Beatles fans!

That entire white bread audience was related to the Von Trapp family! …I was about to upchuck my breakfast.

I closed my eyes and prayed for it to be over…and soon.

And it was.

I was in heaven once again as I was staring in to HUGE fullscreened faces of John, Paul, George, George, George, and Ringo.

Now THAT made everything else worth it!

I had no idea exactly how beautiful George's eyes were until I saw them spread out twenty feet across The Logan Theatre screen.

From there on in, nothing else mattered.

The Beach Boys?…Who?
Leslie Gore?…Sunshine, Lollipops, and What?!

CHAPTER THIRTY

Three weeks after the closed-circuit performance was my sixteenth birthday.

Mom made me an extremely delicious chocolate layer cake, I got a new stereo from my parents, sixteen bucks from my grandmother, Pat took me out to lunch, Aunt Dorothy bought me a charm bracelet, Shelly bought me sixteen new Beatles magazines, and Doris left a note for me on the clothesline— I recognized her handwriting. It was a homemade birthday card, with all of The Beatles faces cut out on it, lovingly attached to my Mom's clothesline right outside our kitchen door. It said:

Happy 16th Birthday
to our BIGGEST FAN!!!!

XOXOXOXO,
John, Paul, George, and Ringo
(but especially George!)

What could be sweeter than that?!

Just as I was about to leave the house and head out for school, Shelly called me. "Hey, remember when you said, the perfect gift would have to have something to do with The Beatles?"

"Yeah."

"And that's why I got you the magazines."

"I know. That was so cool!"

"Well, your wish just made history!"

"What are you talkin' about?"

"Jude...this week, your sixteenth birthday week, The Beatles made record history by holding the top five spots on the charts!"

"What?!"

"Yep."

"How come I didn't hear that?!"

"You need to listen to more radio and give your *Meet The Beatles* album a break!"

I smiled. "What songs made the top five?"

"*Can't Buy Me Love...Twist and Shout...She Loves You... I Want To Hold Your Hand...*and *Please, Please Me.*"

"WHAT A BIRTHDAY!" I squealed with delight.

"You lucky dog! How smooth is that?!"

"I'll say! How smooth is that?!"

Right around that time another album on the Vee-Jay label came out called, *Introducing The Beatles*. Now I had two albums to alternate on my new stereo.

George sang, *Do You Want To Know A Secret?* on this album and I loved it! ...Well, of course I did.

The songs on the latest LP were:

I Saw Her Standing There (Paul)
Misery (John)
Anna (John)

Boys (Ringo)
Love Me Do (Mostly Paul)
P.S. I Love You (Paul) *Baby, It's You* (John)
Do You Want To Know A Secret? (GEORGE!)
A Taste of Honey (Paul)
There's a Place (Mostly John)
And...*Twist and Shout*! (Definitely John)

You know, since The Beatles came into my life, even school seemed to breeze on by for me. I never realized, but being in a good mood all the time, makes just about everything else a lot easier. The 'Clique-y' girls at school didn't annoy me anymore, the bullies never bullied me...even my pain-in-the-ass teachers were less a pain-in-the-ass. High school was a good experience for me from then on because I didn't allow the usual teenage school stuff to get in the way of my other more personal and exciting teenage stuff—The Beatles.

Girls in school were crying over cheating boyfriends, fair-weather friends, and how they hated doing chores at home. The guys were either jocks, bad boys, nerds, or bullies, or those kids just barely gettin' by, for whatever reason. I never gave the jocks, bullies, or bad boys a second thought. I more easily identified with the nerds and the kids who struggled—the underdogs, male or female. Everyone else at school, teachers included, just existed as far as I was concerned. So, I got my work done, kept a low profile, and then zipped on outta school the minute the last bell rang.

I had bigger fish to fry.

CHAPTER THIRTY-ONE

I picked up the telephone to call the world's most famous person for her continued lack of 'continuity of purpose.' "Shelly? Do they have New York and New Jersey Yellow Pages at The Telephone office on Oxford Avenue?"

"I think so. They all do, don't they?"

"I forget. I go in with Mom to pay the bill, but I just look at the new phones, I don't give much attention to anything else."

"So, why do you wanna know that?"

"I have a plan."

"A Beatles-related plan?"

"Is there any other kind?"

The Plot Thickens

That afternoon I was off from work and the minute I scooted out of school I headed down Oxford Avenue straight to the Bell Telephone Office.

It was a really beautiful marble and concrete building. It looked like a stately old bank from the turn of the century.

As I entered I looked around and not far from the bill paying section were rows and rows of telephone books for every state in the union!

Perfect!

I pulled out my notebook, a pen, and then started leafing through the books for hotels in Manhattan and Atlantic City.

"May I help you?" A lovely young woman with a Donna Reed look about her asked me.

"No, thank you. I think I'm okay. It's gonna be a lotta work, but I'll manage."

She smiled at me.

"What time do you close?" I asked.

"At six."

"Six? Oh, well…I can come back."

"Is this something for school?"

"Not really, it's something more for a…a life experience project."

"I see…"

The woman walked away and then turned right around and walked back to me. She put her hand on my shoulder and said, "You know, if you're looking for certain buildings or offices, those numbers and addresses usually stay the same. I believe I have a Manhattan phone book and an Atlantic City phone book in the back—Yellow Pages too. We just throw out those old white and yellow editions. We have to keep it current, even if 99% of everything is the same the next year. So, if they're back there, you can have them if you like."

"Can I? Really?!"

"You most certainly can. Now let me have a look-see."

Donna Reed was gone for about five minutes, and when she came out of the back office, she was smiling broadly, and in her hands were two books, one rather small Atlantic City Yellow Pages and a HUGE Manhattan one.

"Here you are. I hope this helps you with your mission."

I took the two books into my hands and smiled back at her. "Thank you so much! Umm, Miss…?"

Again she smiled. "McGillicutty. Mary McGillicutty."

"You're kidding!"

"No. That's me.

"Miss McGillicutty, this is the *second* time in my life your name has been a blessing to me."

She gave me an odd look.

"It's a long story, Mary. A very, very long story."

CHAPTER THIRTY-TWO

I didn't have to work on Saturday and Sunday, so, I took no phone calls, completed ALL of my homework in less than two hours, and then set my sites on the bigger picture—the summer of 1964.

Right before dinner my mother called out to tell me Shelly was downstairs.

What's she doin' here?

"Hey, you," she said the minute my feet hit the landing.

"Hey you yourself. What are you doing here?"

"I had to work today and I wanted to stop at Bollendorf's for a few new Beatles Magazines, and..."

"And, since you were close by you thought you'd drop in?"

"Somethin' like that," she smiled.

"Shelly? Would you like to stay for dinner?" Mom asked as she put on her apron.

"Sure! I'd love it! Thanks!"

Now I'll give my mother this much—despite the fact that she could be a real thorn in my side, and a genuine pain in my teenage neck, she was one fabulous cook! Credit where credit is due.

"Want me to set the table?" I asked.

"No, that's okay. It's just you and me and Shelly. I'll manage out here."

"Okay."

"I'll call you two when it's ready."

Mom smiled at Shelly and me and then walked back toward the kitchen.

"What are we havin'?" Shelly asked.

"Mom made meatloaf, mashed potatoes, fresh mixed veggies from the garden and home made buttermilk biscuits."

"Mmmmm."

"And, there's a three layer orange sponge cake for dessert," I said as we started to walk upstairs.

"Yummy!"

"I'll say."

The minute we entered my room, *Twist and Shout* from the *Introducing The Beatles* album was just about to end.

"I love this song. Man, John Lennon can sing, can't he?"

I agreed. "I love John's voice."

I changed sides on the album and then situated myself comfortably on my bed in-between the Atlantic City and Manhattan Yellow Pages.

"What's all this stuff?"

"Sit down, Shell. Get ready to hear the best Beatles plan ever."

"What is it?"

"Hand me that alphabetical file, will ya?"

Shelly reached for it on my nightstand.

"I have a 100% guaranteed plan to stay at The Beatles hotels this summer, and no one can turn us away."

"You mean no more Aunt Mary McGillicutty stories?'

"Exactly."

"So what's the plan?"

"Look, we already know where they're gonna be for the August tour, right?"

"Well, we know what cities they're going to."

"Exactly," I smiled handing her the Atlantic City Yellow Pages, "So, all we have to do is write a letter to every big hotel *in* that city and request a reservation for that night."

"What?!"

"Listen, they're gonna be in Atlantic City on August 30th. They have to stay somewhere!"

"And?"

"So, we go through the Atlantic City phone book, write to every hotel there, and ask for reservations for that night. All we need is I.D. and their confirmation letter when we arrive at the hotel. Same thing with New York City. As for Philly? I'll call and make the local reservations. We're in!"

"Oh, my God! That's brilliant! *Brilliant!* You oughta work for Interpol or Scotland Yard or something."

I stood and took a bow.

"Hey, Shell? Can you stay overnight tonight? We could get all this done if you do."

"No sweat. I'll call my Mom."

CHAPTER THIRTY-THREE

Dinner was scrumptious, as always. Shelly and I washed the dishes for Mom, and then, as far as my mother knew, we were upstairs in my room working on an 'after school project.'

Shelly manned the Atlantic City assignment and I took Manhattan.

Shelly had better handwriting than I did and so she wrote the letters while I typed mine on Dad's old Smith-Corona.

Letters to:

The Traymore, Dennis, Claridge, The Ritz-Carlton, Marlborough-Blenheim, The President, The New Yorker, Waldorf-Astoria, Haddon Hall, The Ambassador, The Delmonico, The Lafayette, New York Hilton, The Warwick Hotel, Roosevelt Hotel, The Wellington, Knickerbocker, The Americana, The Ansonia…and The Plaza, (again) because you just never know, and more.

By the time Sunday afternoon rolled around, we were done—five-hundred and ninety-seven prospects in all.

Shelly kept clapping her hands together. "My writing hand feels numb."

I smiled at her. "I'm proud of you, Shell. Your hand might be numb, but you're no longer suffering from a lack of continuity of purpose."

She smiled at me.

We sat there and calculated that we would need exactly twenty-nine dollars and eighty-five cents to mail all of them.

I vowed to mail a hundred off every payday. That would give us plenty of time to receive our answers and it wouldn't break our budgets in the process. Shelly gave me ten dollars to get started.

Again, life was good.

CHAPTER THIRTY-FOUR

It didn't take any time at all before the school year officially ended.

Now I was a Junior in High School.

Summertime allowed me to work a full forty-hour week at the hospital, so I would really be raking in the bucks!

And I'd be needing them: The Beatles concert tickets, staying in their hotel, train fare, bus fare, cab fare, new albums, tickets to their movie, clothes…

Also by mid-June we had already received 418 responses back from possible Beatles hotels welcoming us to stay and if they could be of any further assistance before our arrival, we were to "please telephone."

How perfect was that?!

In the meantime, I had joined three Beatles Fan Clubs, and located seven English pen pals. I kept up regular correspondence with seven great girls, all in different sections of Liverpool. Their names were: Pauline, Julia, Mary, Theresa, Phyllis, Brenda, and Ginny.

I loved getting mail with a Liverpool postmark. It made me feel like a bigger part of the whole Beatles scene. Some of these pen pal girls had seen the Beatles at the Cavern (the local Liverpool haunt that made them famous) over one hundred times and I learned a lot about the boys, their families, and the city itself. They even sent me copies of Mersey Beat magazine to catch up on all the happenings in Liverpool. I was totally absorbed reading my 'fab' and 'gear' magazine in study hall. I mean, it sure beat the pants off of conjugating verbs or reading War and Peace!

One of my pen pals, Ginny, wrote to me (she was a George fan as well) that during the filming of their movie, *A Hard Day's Night*, 'our' George had become smitten with one of the actresses in the film.

I wrote back and said, "Gin, I don't want to hear about it. I'm too young to have a broken heart. I'm chalking it up as a meaningless fling."

Ginny liked the idea of that, too—George lover that she was—and so we made a deal never to talk about 'her' again.

And we didn't.

CHAPTER THIRTY-FIVE

"JUDY!" Shelly hollered into the phone, "*A Hard Day's Night* premieres in Philly on August 11th!"

"Who says?"

"I just heard it on WIBG! It's gonna play in about fifty theaters all around Philly!"

"Oh man, I can't wait to go! I'm there, Baby! I'm there!!!"

"You're goin' to all fifty theaters?!"

I smiled. "That's a little overkill, Shell. Ummm, maybe only forty-eight...forty-nine..."

She laughed. "That sounds about right."

During what little time I had between working forty to fifty hours a week, dreaming about seeing *A Hard Day's Night*, writing to pen pals, strategizing about The Beatles August tour, cleaning my room, washing, ironing, walking the dog, and filing away five-hundred and ninety-seven hotel reservations—alphabetically—I was working on a totally new style for myself.

I was tired of looking like a poster girl for the Oktoberfest. I was tall, five feet eight and a half—a few inches taller than all of my girlfriends. I was blonde, blue-eyed, with a slight gap in-between my front teeth that I actually kinda liked. But there was nothing really special about me, nothing foreign or mysterious.

I toyed with that Ronette idea for the longest time, you know, a BIG heavily sprayed beehive hairdo piled on top of my head in a Bridget Bardot style, with lots of long hair flowing down around my shoulders, and those seductive cat-eyes.

I stopped at Tancredi's Pharmacy on Frankford Avenue one night after work and picked up some black liquid eyeliner and five cans of Aqua Net.

I was a girl on a mission.

Look out world, here comes the fourth Ronette!

The minute I got home I taped a picture of Estelle Bennett, George's favorite Ronette, to the mirror on my chest of drawers.

I carefully opened my black Egyptian eyeliner and started to practice that enticing, cat-eyed, Ronette look. The closest I got was the 'I just went fifteen rounds with Sonny Liston' look.

But, I was a never-say-die kinda kid all of my life, and certainly this time would be no different.

Over the next three days I visited Tancredi's every night after work and eventually cleaned them out of all the black Egyptian eyeliner they had.

And, every night I would lock myself in my room and stare at Estelle's picture. Then, I'd take that eyeliner in my hand, move up as close to the mirror as possible and then it was: practice, practice, practice.

By my 50th attempt I no longer looked like someone punched me in both eyes.

By my 100th I had this lop-sided Cleopatra thing goin' on.

But, by my 200th attempt, I coulda passed for a blonde-haired Ronette!

Perfect!

I was cat-eyed and bee-hived and ready for my close-up, Mr. De Mille...I mean, Mr. Harrison!

That Thursday, I invited Shelly over for dinner. She had to work, so I helped Mom, did my chores, and then ran upstairs, closed the door, and Ronette'd myself.

About 5:30 I heard a knock on my door.

"Hold on!" I shouted.

"Lemme in or I'll huff and I'll puff and I'll blow this door down!"

"Hold your water."

"Jude, it's only me. Open the door!"

"I know, I know! Hold on!"

I checked myself in the mirror. I was a vision—blonde Ronette hair, those seductive cat eyes, a black and turquoise mini-dress and strappy roman sandals. Woo-hoo!

"Hold on, Shell!" I called out one more time as I gave my hair just one last spritz of Aqua Net.

Then, I moved to my left so that Shelly couldn't see me until the door closed behind her.

I clicked the key in the lock, she turned around and then...

"OH, MY GOD! YOU...UH...UH...I MEAN..."

"Calm down, Shell."

"Your...your parents are gonna kill you! Look at you! OH, MY GOD! Are you INSANE?!"

"Cut the drama," I said poofing my beehive one more time.

"Drama?! Look who's talkin'! And *where* did you get that dress?!"

"Rual's on Frankford Avenue. You like it?"

"Well, yeah, it's...it's kinda cute."

"And?"

"And *where*," she said pointing to my feet. "did you get those… those Spartacus sandals? I know you didn't get *them* on Frankford Avenue!"

"I bought them in Center City. And *look*, Shell…" I moved my hair to the side, "silver hoop earrings!"

"You got your ears pierced?!"

"Priscilla Hannah did them for me at work. They're all healed up."

"Oh, my God, that's crazy!"

I smiled, "Crazy? Hey, wait 'til you see my tattoo!"

"WHAT?! You got a…"

"I didn't get a tattoo," I laughed.

"You've lost it. You really and truly have. My God, I feel like I'm gonna pass out."

"Alright, alright look…settle down. Just get over that it's me and where I bought this stuff, and tell me what you think."

"I *think* you look like an underage go-go dancer from The Peppermint Lounge!"

"You say that like it's a bad thing."

"I'm *saying*, what in God's name ever possessed you to…"

Then she moved up closer to me and really examined the 'eye work.'

"Wow, how did you do that? They look… perfect."

CHAPTER THIRTY-SIX

"You'd better get a shower, get the makeup off, and lose the hairdo, or your ass is grass. Your Mom said dinner would be ready by 6:00."

"I got time."

"Yeah, if you hurry."

I grabbed a pair of pajamas, my robe and slippers and then headed for the bathroom. Thank God it was right next door to my bedroom.

It was pretty easy to get the eye makeup off, but man, that hairspray was like Elmer's glue! I had to wash my hair three times and then put extra crème rinse on just so I could pull a comb through it. Yet, by the time it was 5:55 I was sitting in front of my hair dryer, looking absolutely no worse for wear. What that meant was, the Oktoberfest poster girl was back in full force. I wasn't too happy about my old wholesome look, but, somewhere deep inside me was the underage go-go dancer from The Peppermint Lounge, so, everything was just fine by me.

Shelly and I walked into the dining room and Mom had prepared another great spread for dinner: pork roast, browned potatoes and carrot pennies, gravy, fresh biscuits and a home made lemon meringue pie for dessert. As I said before, Mom was quite the cook!

The conversation at the dinner table was the usual:

"How's school?"

"How's work?"

"Dinner is delicious."

Lah-de-dah, lah-de-dah.

After we finished our wonderful meal we helped Mom with the cleanup and then we were free for the evening. Shelly and I spent the night discussing the concerts we were going to and the best chance of being able to meet them once we were inside their hotel.

The dates were set: August 28th and 29th at Forest Hills Stadium, August 30th at Convention Hall, Atlantic City, and September 2nd right on our own home turf in Philly at Convention Hall.

Four Beatles concerts in less than a week!

My bet was on Atlantic City as our best chance.

"How come not here in Philly?" Shelly seemed a bit confused.

"Shell," I said, "Atlantic City is much smaller, and The Democratic National Convention is there that week and so is The Miss America Pageant."

"So?"

"So…those cops'll be too pooped out to want to chase a bunch of crazed Beatles fans all over the place."

"I see your point."

"I thought you would."

"Hey…can I ask you another question?"

"Sure."

"How are you gonna get that Ronette outfit out of the house. You can't leave here lookin' like that!"

"Shelly," I said in a sweet yet patronizing way, "you just leave the brain work to me."

*An ad from the Philadelphia Inquirer promoting "A Hard Day's Night."
Notice the Ellis movie theatre, where Judy saw the film. She saw it
57 times that summer.*

CHAPTER THIRTY-SEVEN

Oh, what love can do. The ever-hard-working soul that I was did a complete turnabout and I took three days in a row off from work.

WHY?

So I could spend those three days in the movie theater watching *A Hard Day's Night.*

The only reason Miss Barley, the office manager at the hospital, gave them to me was because prior to asking I worked nine days straight and eleven extra hours overtime. She knew she had a good worker on her hands, so she decided to give me what I wanted—as was my plan from the get-go.

I actually told my parents the truth, and since they were both movie buffs, and realized I couldn't possibly get into any trouble watching The Beatles along with a few hundred other girls, they were okay with it.

Imagine that!

Shelly, on the other hand, made a BIG mistake. She took off three days too, but never told her parents. She might have gotten away with it, but Grant's 5 & 10 Cent store called her house and wanted to check to see if it was three or four days she requested off from work.

Mrs. Winkler, the store manager, didn't get to ask Shelly that question. She asked her mother; who just happened to pick up the phone first.

Shelly then told her parents the truth but it was just too late for them to feel anything but anger that their daughter was trying to pull one over on them.

So, the very first time I saw *A Hard Day's Night*, I saw it alone.

Pat was babysitting, Doris wasn't allowed to go, and a few other girls I knew from school were going to see the movie, but at the theaters closer to where they lived.

I walked into the Ellis Theater on Frankford Avenue and there were Beatles posters everywhere. The *Hard Day's Night* movie ads displayed four shaggy heads only from their eyes up, but there wasn't even one girl in the theater who couldn't tell you who was who. Well, of course, we were Beatles fans!

A booming voice spoke from the back of the movie house, "The film will be starting in five minutes! Please be seated."

I bought a large popcorn and a Coke, walked over to get a box of Goobers, and just as I passed the telephones on the way to my seat, I turned around, placed my treats on the floor next to me and put a dime into the pay phone. Quickly I dialed: GArfield 6-2832. Shelly answered.

"I thought you'd be at the movies by now," she said sadly.

"I am. I'm at The Ellis."

"So why are you calling me?" she sighed.

Just then the usual ads for refreshments started to play and I said to my friend, "Shell… hold on. Can you hear this?"

I pulled the phone cord out as far as it would go and pointed it in the direction of the screen's speakers. I waited until one advertisement was over and then put the phone back up against my ear. "Didja hear that?"

"I heard some people singing, *Hop on down to the popcorn stand*? You mean that?"

"Yup."

"Jude, what are you up to now?"

"Listen to me. I can see the screen just fine and if you can hear it just fine, well…I'll just stand here and hold the phone for you so you can at least *hear* the movie!"

"What? For ninety minutes?!"

"Look, I know it's not like seeing their faces, but you'll recognize their voices, you can put a face to the voice."

"And you'd do that for me?!"

"Sure I would."

"Jude, you're a real goofball sometimes, but you gotta good heart. I'll give ya that much."

"So, are ya ready?"

The smile was back in Shelly's voice. "I'm ready!"

Just then a grey, black, and white sign that said UNITED ARTISTS quietly filled the large screen.

And then, TWANG!!!!!!!!!!!! *A Hard Day's Night* started to play and there they were, full screen, running around the streets of London chased by hundreds and hundreds of fans!

I felt like I was right there running along with them!

And, in a very odd way…so did Shelly.

CHAPTER THIRTY-EIGHT

By the time Shelly was off house arrest, I had already seen *A Hard Day's Night* fifteen times. By the time I saw *eight* features I could recite the entire opening scene of the movie by heart. (I've always been a quick study.) Shelly would call me on the phone just to ask me to repeat it in my now very good Liverpudlian accent.

I must have recited those lines to Shelly about three dozen times, and, by the time she actually saw the movie, she could recite it word for word herself.

In less than three weeks we were ready to see our boys once again in person and I had seen the film thirty-two times, and Shelly—just over a dozen.

If I never saw another bag of popcorn or a box of Goobers again, it would be waaaaaay too soon for me.

CHAPTER THIRTY-NINE

August 27, 1964
7:16 AM
Wakeling Street

"**S**HELLY!!!" I hollered into the telephone, "The Beatles are staying at The Delmonico!"

"Oh, my God! Did you check the reservation file? Was that one of the hotels you wrote to?"

"Shell," I said, with a smile as cool as the Cheshire Cat's, "listen to this…

'Thank you for requesting reservations here at The Delmonico for the night of August 28th, 1964.

We are confirming a rate for a twin suite @ $21.00 per night.

Should you require any additional services or special accommodations, please feel free to contact us.'

And, it's got the official signature, and the address, and…we are sooooo in!!!"

"My God! You're brilliant!"

I nodded. "Well, I have my moments."

"Where's The Delmonico?"

"Park Avenue and 59th."

"And all we have to do is…"

"Shelly, all we have to do is pack a bag and walk into the hotel."

"What I.D. are you bringing?"

"I've got my passport and school I.D."

"I don't have a passport."

"So what! Just bring your school identification."

This time both of us were smart and we told our parents we really wanted to go to New York to see The Beatles and for some reason, our honesty won out. We promised to call from the hotel when we got there and again after the concert.

The hotel was in a very 'high end' section of the city, well-guarded and safe, and so we were allowed to spread our wings, hop on the bus, and enjoy two days of The Beatles before we were off to Atlantic City on the 30th.

We'd be home for two more days and then we'd see them again at Convention Hall in Philly on September 2nd.

I carefully packed my jammies, green miniskirt outfit with matching top, my black and turquoise mini dress and Spartacus sandals, shampoo, crème rinse, Aqua Net, lipstick, toothpaste, toothbrush, and black Egyptian eyeliner into the small, white round Samsonite suitcase I got for my thirteenth birthday.

I also placed the very precious million-dollar Delmonico reservation letter inside a special compartment within the luggage.

Shelly packed in a similar fashion, just minus a 'mini' anything, and definitely no Egyptian eyeliner from Tancredi's.

My Dad drove us down to 13th and Filbert to catch the bus.
"You kids have fun! Be safe! And say hello to Bingo for me!"
"Dad…it's Ringo!"
"Oh, Bingo, Ringo, what's the difference?"
Again…parents are clueless.

CHAPTER FORTY

August 28, 1964
2:00 PM
New York City

We arrived at The Delmonico by taxi at 2:00 PM. It was pandemonium! There had to be at least ten thousand girls surrounding the place.

The cabbie drove as close to the hotel as possible and Shelly and I and two small pieces of Samsonite luggage made it through the crowd like we were storming the beaches at Normandy.

Every time a cop, on horseback or on foot, tried to stop us, I was adamant that we had reservations, and for some reason (my being adamant?) no one asked to see them. I was kinda glad that they didn't because if any one of those ten thousand girls had gotten their hands on it, we woulda been sunk!

When Shelly and I reached higher ground, we were questioned a bit more thoroughly and I felt okay about opening my luggage to show hotel doormen, staff, and a few policemen our ID and hotel reservation.

Upon thorough inspection, a policeman named Harrison, oddly enough, gave a nod to the doorman who then said, "Welcome to The Delmonico, Ladies."

We walked to the reservation desk, paid for our room and then we were handed a key. To me, that key was not only to open the door to our room, it was a legitimate open invitation to explore all of the hotel—Beatles floor included.

The Delmonico.

What a grand hotel!

Elegant, stylish…

When we arrived, I found out that our dear Ed Sullivan actually lived there all year round. The hotel was his home! Lucky Ed.

Shelly and I had a beautiful room with two twin beds on the fifth floor.

The Beatles had a suite of rooms just three floors above us.

We were in the best situation possible, but it was still a hassle. Every time Shelly and I walked outside our room or took an elevator anywhere we were asked for ID and our room key. Police would call the front desk and escort us back to our room as if we were prisoners. We were dragged down to the management office, to Security, to the Concierge…. It was a nightmare. In fact, the fifth time we were brought down to the Concierge, the man felt so bad for the two of us that he offered his most sincere apologies and then offered us dinner, anything and everything at all that we wanted.

"Room service?" Shelly asked.

"Yes, indeed, young lady, if that's what you would prefer."

I nodded. "Room service sounds great!"

Shelly and I left the lobby and then decided a good free meal under our belt might not be such a bad idea.

We ordered two steaks—medium well, baked potatoes with sour cream and chives, corn on the cob, fresh biscuits, chocolate mousse pie, milk, tea, and two Cokes.

Then, the Concierge sent someone from housekeeping up to our room and gifted Shelly and myself with the official Delmonico Hotel robe. A beautiful white, fluffy Turkish bath robe. I loved it! We were also offered a limousine for the evening, if we had a specific place in mind—"A Broadway show, perhaps... maybe some shopping?"

I chuckled a bit into the telephone and said, "Well, Sir...we were just...just given tickets to The Beatles concert out in Queens tonight, but I guess that would be asking too much and..."

"Not too much to ask at all, Miss. It's a very small thing to do considering the way you were treated today, and again, we at The Delmonico apologize."

"Well, thank you..." I was speechless—for once.

The Concierge told me not to give it another thought. Our limousine would be waiting for us at 7:15 and when the concert was over, the driver would pick us up at the same spot we were dropped off.

Lady Luck continued to smile upon us.

CHAPTER FORTY-ONE

We were escorted like royalty to the downstairs garage where four beautiful, shiny black limousines waited. Shelly and I ran toward the closest car, a driver opened the door for us and we got in. Not ten seconds into our seats, a police officer instructed us to go to the first limousine…and so we obliged.

"My God!! These other limos are for The Beatles! I just know it!"

Shelly turned to look at me, turned back to look at the limos, and then back to me again. "No. These *can't* be! Didn't someone say they were taking a helicopter to Forrest Hills?"

"Shell," I smiled. "They have to get to the helicopter first."

Our driver started to pull away and all Shelly and I could do was look out the back window toward the other limousines. Just as we were about to turn the corner to exit the parking garage we saw four shaggy haired men enter the limo that we had previously occupied.

I pushed my face as close to the back window as possible and I was 100 gazillion percent positive I saw Paul and Ringo about to enter the limo on the driver's side. "Shelly, look!!!"

"RINGO!!!! THERE'S MY RINGO!!!!" she squealed in-between laughing and crying and crying and laughing. "I SAW HIM!!! I SAW HIM!!!!! Oh, My God, Jude! The Beatles are in our limousine!!! They can smell our Chanel No. 5!!!"

"We're gettin' closer all the time, Shell. …Closer *all* the time."

CHAPTER FORTY-TWO

Forrest Hills Stadium was a mad house. 16,000 die-hard Beatles fans in a frenzy.

Apparently, I wasn't the only one who had plotted and fine-tuned some strategies since the boys' last trip to America. The stadium people did a pretty good job themselves—an eight-foot tall barbed-wire fence not only to keep fans out of harm's way, but out of The Beatles' way, too!

And New York Girls?

We're talkin' tough.

Oh, yeah.

When we got to our seats, we heard that one girl named Angie had somehow managed to get Ringo's St. Christopher Medal right off his neck! Then, later on, she got to meet him and kiss him, with photographers swarming all over the two of them when she gave the medal back to good old Ringo. And it all happened right there at The Delmonico, too! Shelly was heartsick over it.

What luck that Angie girl had!

Well, maybe not luck, but…oh, you know what I mean.

As for *our* luck, we never mentioned our limo ride to the girls seated next to us, or about seeing the boys in The Delmonico garage, or even that we were actually staying there at the hotel.

That was our little secret.

The show started late that night because we heard that the helicopter pilot didn't get proper permission or something and because of it the show was delayed 'til almost 10:00 PM. But that was okay, we made new friends, and we talked about our favorite Beatle, *A Hard Day's Night*, and the concert we were about to see.

But we were immediately reprogrammed when The Beatles took the stage, and a roar of such monumental proportion erupted that it's hard to explain. I guess you can chalk that up to one of those times when "you just had to be there."

From *Twist and Shout* to *Long Tall Sally*, 16,000 Beatles fans, including yours truly and Shelly, got a taste of heaven.

Thirty-one minutes later, the concert was over, and the boys were gone, but I could still hear the buzz of leftover music in my ears.

Shelly and I ran out of the stadium as fast as we could, so we'd make it back to the hotel around the same time The Beatles got there.

Our limousine driver saw us coming, opened the doors, and off we went back into the City…back to The Delmonico…and The Beatles.

CHAPTER FORTY-THREE

It was a lot easier going back to The Delmonico than the first time we walked into the hotel—thanks to a direct stadium-to-hotel limousine and the parking garage entrance.

The minute we got to our room I hopped in the shower, dried off, and then started to 'Ronette' my hair and eyes.

Shelly got in the shower right after I was finished, and by the time she came out, I had already dried my hair and was in the first stage of 'bee-hiving.'

"You know," she said staring at me. "I used to curse my curly hair, but now that I see what you have to go through to do this 'Estelle' thing, I'm not complainin' anymore."

"Hah! The hair is nothing!" I said, "It takes me three times as long to get my eyes right."

"Well, you're tenacious, I'll give you that much. Crazy, but tenacious."

By the time Shelly had changed into her black pencil skirt, and pretty white Edwardian blouse, I was in my black and turquoise mini dress, and Spartacus sandals, complete with Ronette hair, cat eyes, and big silver hoop earrings.

I opened the door to our room and smiled, "It's showtime!"

CHAPTER FORTY-FOUR

Well, in a nutshell, our plans went awry and it was a total washout. You know the road to hell, good intentions, and all that.

The closest we got to the Beatles was a reporter who had just interviewed them a bit earlier in the hotel's Crystal Ballroom. He made a grungy pass at me, and it was scary.

Shelly was less than sympathetic. "That's what you get, Miss Hot Stuff."

"Hey! I should be able to look cool and not get hit on in such a graphic manner."

"Well, true. At least you knew how to shut him up."

"Yeah, the 'I'm only sixteen' thing seemed to work pretty well, didn't it?"

"Yeah, it did."

Shelly and I decided right then to go back to our room and make other plans. It was well after midnight, so we didn't have too much time left…and we knew it.

I brainstormed and called the front desk to tell them that a rather expensive-looking package had been left at our door for

Mr. George Harrison and it said 'personal' so could he please come down to get it.

Ten minutes later a knock came on our door, and I thought I would faint.

I grabbed the doorknob slowly, poofed my Ronette hair just one more time, and then smiled at Shelly.

"George," I whispered.

Then I opened the door, and there he was!!!!

CHAPTER FORTY-FIVE

"THE BELLBOY!" I shrieked. "Ummm, yes, Miss. I... I was told there was something special here to pick up for Mr. Harrison."

Shelly laughed, "Sure! You got a baggage rack for her to sit on?"

I gave her a dirty cat-eyed look. "Very funny."

Now, what am I gonna do?!
Think fast, Jude! Think fast!

I walked over to the small writing desk and picked up the box of assorted chocolates that the hotel had left on our dinner tray.

"Please tell Mr. Harrison, I hope he enjoys them." I handed the Bellboy the candy, I smiled, and then closed the door.

Shelly turned the covers down on her bed and pointed to the alarm clock. "Jude, look, it's almost 2:00 AM. Why don't we just get some sleep and try this crazy stuff again after breakfast."

I yawned. "Yeah, I guess. We've got another whole day here and then there's still Atlantic City and Philly!"

"Atta girl."

"But…"

"Now what?"

"I was just thinkin'."

"Oh, God. What is it?"

"Maybe just…just one more phone call before I un-Ronette myself."

"This is insane! It's too late! Nothin's gonna happen now. Go to sleeeeep!"

I picked up the telephone and in my BEST English accent I asked to be connected to The Beatles Suite because I was missing my silver bracelet and the latch might have broken when I was up there and…

Shelly nodded. "Good one."

"Just a moment please," a sweet voice said.

Within three seconds a man answered in a wild, fast, and funny accent, "Hi-low! Yuv reached Beasties Central. Surrey, but Job Lemon is aiding his three beast pills and wit a sour face as well…"

I heard a familiar Liverpudlian laugh and then the line disconnected.

I sat there with my mouth hanging open.

"Who was it?!" Shelly had to know. "Who was it?!!!"

I could still hear his laugh in my head, as I scribbled every word I recalled him saying on the hotel stationery.

"JUDE! Was it George? NO? HUH? Was it Ringo? Bingo? Paul?"

I flopped back on the bed, "Oh, my God!"

Shelly was now in full panic mode. "What?! WHAT?!! WHAT IS IT?!!!"

"I just talked to Job Lemon!!!"

CHAPTER FORTY-SIX

August 29, 1964
6:15 AM
The Delmonico

Shelly and I woke up to the sound of an ear-stinging alarm clock that read 6:15. A few seconds later a wake-up call arrived.

I politely and very sleepily said, "Thank you."

"Why did you ask for that call?" Shelly said as she stretched herself awake. "We had the alarm."

"For back up. You can never be too sure."

She nodded. "How did you sleep?"

"Like a rock. How about you?"

Shelly smiled, "Like two rocks. I was dreaming about Ringo."

I smiled back at her.

We showered and ordered breakfast. We were paying for this one, so it was far less the splendid fare than our gift from the hotel a day earlier.

One large pot of coffee, two glasses of OJ, and two croissants later, we were ready to start out our second, 'We're gonna meet The Beatles Day!'

Before I got wrapped up in anything else, I called the Concierge and asked if we could check out a bit later in the day.

He said, "Yes."

I also asked if we could leave our bags at the desk and come back to pick them up on our way home later that evening—around 11:30 or so.

Again, he said, "Yes."

I decided to hold off on the Ronette look until we were in Atlantic City. Shelly also gave way on the tight pencil skirt in favor of a more Mod and colorful A-line shift dress, and I wore my green (not too short) mini outfit that I had worn to the concert the night before.

I figured, maybe I could get lucky with the old wholesome Oktoberfest look this time.

Maybe.

CHAPTER FORTY-SEVEN

Timing is everything, and as good as our timing was at The Delmonico, things just really didn't pan out.

On three more occasions we were taken to the Concierge's desk, and then the same old sleazy reporter saw us in the hallway on our way back to our room, and he hit on me again!

"Doesn't the age sixteen strike you as off limits?"

Shelly nudged him and said, "Look, buddy, there's enough cops in this hotel to see that you get your butt kicked right on outta here."

"Yeah," I agreed, "Get lost, you crud."

Just then two gentlemen who smelled positively wonderful walked by us and into the elevator not two feet away from where we stood.

"Are you ladies alright?" one of them asked.

"Yessir, we're fine," I smiled. "He was just leaving."

The elevator door closed, took the gentlemen along with it, and then Shelly said to the resident pervert, "Get lost, or we'll call the cops."

Needless to say, the man took our warning seriously and scooted to the nearest elevator to make his exit.

Suddenly Shelly and I looked at each other and remembered the two men who were about to come to our aid, and we said in unison, "MY GOD! THAT WAS BRIAN EPSTEIN AND ED SULLIVAN!"

Timing really IS everything, and we didn't have much of it those two days in Manhattan. But we sure did have fun!

Shelly and I decided to count our blessings and be grateful for the good that DID happen at The Delmonico rather than the dreams we had that didn't come true. That evening's concert was again a piece of heaven, and we were thrilled to be a part of it.

My mind was immediately in overdrive the second Paul finished the last song of the evening.

Two concerts down and two to go.

Shelly and I said farewell to Forrest Hills memories and took a cab back into the City. We picked up our luggage at The Delmonico, and then headed to Port Authority bus station.

And then…home.

CHAPTER FORTY-EIGHT

August 30, 1964
7:00 AM
At Home on Wakeling Street...for now

Three days after The Democratic National Convention, The Beatles invaded Atlantic City for one stupendous concert at Convention Hall.

Over 19,000 tickets were sold, and two of them were ninth row center and they belonged to me and Shelly!

Once again, thank God for Glassman's. The original seats we bought were for the balcony, but...for just an extra $12.50 I would be sitting just twenty feet away from George Harrison.

Worth every penny.

And thank God for my ingenuity because we also had reservations at The Lafayette Motor Inn! Much to our disappointment, The Beatles had no hotel plans for Philadelphia. The boys were moving right along to their next concert city direct from Philly's airport, so, Atlantic City was my last chance.

Shelly and I woke up around 7:00 AM.

Mom was already in the kitchen making us a good breakfast because she wanted to hear about all the fun we had in New York before we took off again for the shore.

Of course, we left out quite a few details, but all in all she seemed rather pleased that we were so well liked there at The Delmonico that we were given hotel robes. (If she only knew.)

I gifted Mom with my luxurious Turkish robe, and she was over the moon. Then she handed each of us a plateful of pancakes and sausages, and we were equally happy.

See how it all works out?

CHAPTER FORTY-NINE

O nce again, luggage in hand, Shelly and I trekked down Wakeling Street to catch the 59 bus, to catch the El, to catch another bus, that would take us directly into Atlantic City and to The Lafayette Motor Inn—The Last Chance Ranch.

By 9:30 AM we were on the old Greyhound and just before noon we were arriving in Atlantic City—the place of my birth.

I figured that might be a good omen, too.

It was a typical hot and sticky August day even though there was a breeze coming off the Atlantic Ocean. Shelly and I decided to take a cab to The Lafayette so we wouldn't look a sweaty mess by the time we got there.

When we arrived at The Motor Inn, once again, there were girls everywhere!

We stood on the corner for a while so I could get a 'take' on the place.

"Well," I said to Shelly, "for one, it sure is smaller than The Delmonico."

She nodded, "That's a plus."

The crowd was thick, but it was also a lot more friendly than the 'let's rip 'em to shreds' mentality outside The Delmonico.

The small lodge across the street was obviously housing some Beatles fans and they had their radios hanging out the windows, some girls were singing, and some were even line dancing right there in the street. The first song I heard was Martha and the Vandellas—*Dancin' in the Street.*

How perfect!

As Shelly and I made our way to the front of The Lafayette we were dancing right along with the rest of the girls. In fact, I think it actually helped us get to the front of The Inn a lot safer and faster.

Naturally, we were stopped and questioned and questioned and stopped. I pulled out my reservation, passport, and school I.D., so did Shelly.

And, as easy as that…we were in!

CHAPTER FIFTY

The street girls were smart. By the time we made it to the front desk to pay for our room, we already knew that The Beatles were staying on the top floor, that The White House Hoagie Shop was delivering the boys a three-foot long, 'Welcome to Atlantic City' hoagie, and that Jackie DeShannon was playing a game of Monopoly with George!

"Monopoly? With George!" I shook my head.

"Relax, it's just a game," Shelly said as we moved into the elevator.

"But it's a game about the streets of the place where I was born! If anybody should be playin' that game with George, it should be me!"

The elevator bell rang and suddenly we were on the fourth floor—our floor.

"Jude, for a fun gal, this really isn't worth gettin' yourself into a tizzy. You've got bigger fish to fry, remember?"

I put the key into the door, "Yeah...bigger fish."

We freshened up, put our clothes out for the concert, and then checked out the street scene from our fourth-floor window.

Again, girls were everywhere!

Shelly and I strategized and then vowed that we would keep a low profile that afternoon. We'd spend that time walking around The Inn, talking to people, seeing and hearing what we could and causing no problems for anyone.

Polite, discreet, and laid-back were the key words for the day.

But, after we got back from the show, and it was Ronette time? Well, that would be a different story.

CHAPTER FIFTY-ONE

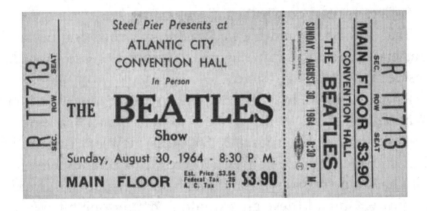

I was only an infant when I traveled across the bridge from The Garden State and into The City of Brotherly Love, so I was always classified as a Philly girl.

In the summertime, Mom, Dad, and I were regular visitors to the Jersey shore, and I loved it: ocean breezes, beautiful sunsets, nice, quiet, peaceful…

But on August 30th, 1964?

Nice?

Quiet?

Peaceful?

Not even close.

Shelly and I stayed true to our promise and even when we did see their manager, Brian Epstein, or any of the other Beatles' entourage, we either said nothing at all, or merely nodded a hello.

Talk about restraint!

But we didn't want Brian, Derek, Mal, or Neil, to remember us as troublemakers—and we really weren't. But the chances of being straight up and honest and saying, "Hi! I'm a big fan and I'd just like to get George's autograph and give him a hug" and having it actually happen, were slim and none.

So, a girl's gotta do whatta girl's gotta do.

That said, Shelly and I stayed true to our vows and behaved ourselves the entire day. We figured the more we got to know the inside of the hotel—the better.

Around 7:15 we left The Lafayette and walked over to Convention Hall to check things out. It was wall-to-wall Beatles fans!

There had to be at least 20,000 girls between The Motor Inn and the venue. The frenzied crowd terrified Shelly, but all I had to do was remind her that back at the hotel, it would be just us and all these girls wouldn't matter one bit. We sat through the opening acts, Jackie DeShannon, Clarence 'The Frogman' Henry, and we were polite...but we wanted The Beatles!

Now, sometimes you get what you wish for, and sometimes you get what you pay for. August 30th was one of those nights that we got what we wished for AND paid for.

Those seats put us smack dab in front of George, and then, there sat Ringo right behind him on a raised platform of some sort. It was FABULOUS!

We had a blast! Singing along, dancing, screaming, singing along, dancing...you get the idea.

And The Beatles had fun that night, too!

I could see it on their faces.

Ringo was constantly smiling and shaking his shaggy head. And it always looked as if there was a private joke going on between John and Paul because they'd continually laugh or smile at each other. George did his cute little footwork and he'd smile that beautiful, crooked smile of his, he'd look shy at times, stomp his feet to the music, and he played his guitar with all of his heart and soul.

The concert was over far too soon, and it took us longer to get back to the hotel than the time we spent at The Hall. But it was divine! All of it.

Again, back at 'The Last Chance Ranch' we were calm and polite. Earlier in the day we made sure the doorman and office people knew our faces so that it was an "Okay" when we tried to step back inside The Lafayette after the concert.

Just as we were entering The Motor Inn, a girl screamed, "They're gonna watch *A Hard Day's Night* tonight!"

"What?!"

I never heard her holler to me again, so I turned to the first official-looking person I saw and said, "Someone said that we're going to see *A Hard Day's Night* tonight?"

He shook his head. "It's a private showing."

"Here?"

"Yes, Miss."

"So, just The Beatles and their entourage and..."

"Yes, Miss. It's a private showing for them exclusively."

"I see. Well, that's nice. Thank you."

Shelly and I headed for the elevator.

"Did you hear that?!" I asked her.

"How could I miss it?"

"Shell, no one watches a movie with the lights on! Who'd know if we were in there? We just have to get to the screening room, and then… we're in! In! In! In! At the Motor Inn!"

We hurried to our room, showered, and dressed.

Shelly and I updated our age a bit with a little help from our friends: cool clothes, Aqua Net, and black Egyptian eyeliner.

"You look GREAT!" I said to Shelly.

"But am I 'Ringo great'?" she asked.

"Yes, indeed you are. Now, me!" I turned around in all of my Ronette glory, in that black and turquoise mini dress I so loved. "Well?"

"Jude, George won't even remember who Pattie Boyd is when he takes a look at you!"

"Hey! Remember? We don't mention that name!"

"What name?"

"The Pattie name."

"Oh, yeah…well, you never heard it from me."

Shelly and I took a walk down into the lobby and all of a sudden, we were surrounded by at least two-dozen women. Nice looking girls, too. Pretty clothes, pretty jewelry…

A very well-dressed gentleman turned to me and said, "You look wonderful! You'll get picked."

I smiled. "Well, that's great!" I turned to Shelly and whispered, "Get picked for what?"

Then I saw a policeman eyeing me and he said, "How old are you?"

I stood up straight and smiled. "I'm fifty-three, but I've aged really well."

A few of the nearby girls laughed.

Shelly was tugging my arm. "Let's get outta here."

I pulled my arm away. "These are nice women. *And* they appreciate my sense of humor—which is more than I can say for you." I smiled back at the girls, and they smiled back at me.

Shelly kept tugging my arm. "We gotta get outta here!"

"Stop that! What is your problem?!"

Just then one of the elevators opened and the girls filed in right behind the nice gentleman in the pinstriped suit. "I'll be down for the rest of you momentarily."

Shelly really yanked at my arm, and she hurt me.

"What the hell is wrong with you?! They're obviously guests for the screening! We're in!"

"Jude," she whispered, "they're hookers."

"Of course they're lookers, why would they want ugly girls up there?"

"Jude…I said hookers, not lookers. Those girls are h-o-o-k-e-r-s! Hookers!"

"Oh, my God!" I said turning quickly and knocking over a large lobby ashtray in the process, "We gotta get outta here!"

"Hey! Pick up that ashtray!" A cop yelled at me.

But I was already flying up the stairwell heading for our room with Shelly running right behind me. By the time we reached Room 403, I was in tears, and I flopped right onto the bed.

"Boys will be boys, Jude."

"But it's not right!"

"Lotsa stuff ain't right, Judy."

"Well, George can't be doin' that. He has Pattie!"

"Oh, NOW you're on Pattie's side!" she smiled.

I sniffled a bit and then carefully made sure when I dried my eyes that the 'Ronette' look was still intact.

"Alright, forget Pattie. So, now what?" I said, straightening my dress.

"Hey, you're the genius plot maker around here, not me."

"Well, then, I say we get back in that elevator and head to the Toppermost of the Poppermost."

"Okay. We're in this together," she smiled. "Let's do it!"

CHAPTER FIFTY-TWO

When we reached the top floor, we were immediately greeted by two very unfriendly-looking Atlantic City policemen.

"How'd you get up here?" one growled at me.

"I pushed the right button, just like you did." I smiled.

"You're guests here?" the other questioned.

"Yes, we are. Room 403. Call the front desk if you like."

And he did.

"Well, apparently you check out okay. So, why are you two here? On *this* particular floor?"

I made a bold move. "Well, we're certainly not here with the hookers. We're local fan club Presidents and we were invited to the private screening."

"It's exclusive." Shelly nudged.

Again, we got the 'eye'—but in a different way—and I was beginning to think he was ready to call our bluff.

The second officer got a call and left us immediately while Sherlock Holmes walked up the hallway to talk to three other cops.

We had no other choice but to try the room doors, if it was the screening room, it would have to be open, and we'd get in. This was our last chance.

Shelly quickly ran to the right and I ran to the left.

Door after door I shook and so did Shelly—and all of them were locked.

Just then, I saw Sherlock wave to us and say, "Okay! The screening's up here, ladies! You're clear!"

BUT we'd already screwed up...and this guy was no dumb bunny, and Sherlock could see exactly what we were doing and that we had obviously, if only for a short while, really pulled the wool over his eyes.

"HEY! YOU TWO!!!"

"SHELLY! RUN! RUUUUN!!!!!!" I called out to her.

I opened the stairwell entrance and flew down those steps like a bat outta hell. I know the cops nailed Shelly right away because I heard her hollering, "HELP! JUDY! HELP! RINGOOO!"

By the time I made it downstairs, Shelly and three policemen were already waiting for me outside Room 403. One immediately turned to me and said, "This is the end of the road for you and your friend here—the other Vandella."

I straightened my skirt and poofed my hair and said in a calm yet winded voice, "That's Ronette, not Vandella."

"Look, smart-ass," the cop said, "I don't care if you're Wilma Flintstone and she's Betty Rubble. You two are outta here!"

"Oh, no! What will Fred and Barney say?!"

"Listen you..."

Shelly's voice quickly interrupted, "Officer, excuse me, but we do have reservations here!"

"And this hotel has rules and regulations and you two broke 'em!"

Shell's eyes started to fill. "Where will we go?"

"How about home? Yeah, why don't you two troublemakers just go home?"

Shelly and I were quickly ushered into our room and in nothing flat we packed up our suitcases—reluctantly.

As soon as we finished, Officer Stern (how fitting) led us to the lobby and then to the front exit. And so, for the second time within a six-month period, I was told to "GET OUT AND STAY OUT!"

There were only about two hundred girls remaining outside The Lafayette when we got the boot. A few walked over and asked what was up, but we didn't even have the words to describe what had happened to us.

It was just sad.

Shelly and I took a slow walk around the block considering our fate.

"Maybe we should just go home."

"I can't, Shell. This is my dream!"

"Well, at this point it's more like my nightmare. We're lucky they didn't arrest us!"

"All I wanted was a date with George. Sheesh, I'da been happy for just a game of Monopoly. I *hate* Jackie DeShannon!"

"I know, Jude."

"I wasn't askin' for much. Just a little conversation, maybe he'd treat me to lunch…buy me a candy bar or something, nothin' elaborate."

"I know."

I lifted my head to the heavens and shouted, "God! Just some conversation! A little one on one. I don't need anything fancy schmancy. ARE YOU LISTENING?!!!"

"Jude, all prayers are answered, but sometimes the answer is no."

"Stop that! The answer is yes! It's gonna happen!"

"Listen, I may lack continuity of purpose, but YOU are a wild, off the wall, harebrained, optimist!"

I smiled at her. "Flattery will get you nowhere."

Shelly and I kept walking and eventually returned to our old stomping grounds, this time in the back of The Lafayette.

As I looked up at the building, I noticed that all the rooms had tiny balconies.

"Balconies, Shelly!"

"What are you talkin' about?"

"We could make it back upstairs again if we could move from one balcony to the next. It's just like the rings in gym class, only…"

"Only what? Deadly?!"

"Shell…look how easy this would be!"

"Easy for who? Zippy the Chimp?!"

"Come on…and even if we don't make it…"

"IF?!!" she shrieked.

"Listen," I said, "if we got stuck on someone's balcony, the newspaper people would be here in a heartbeat! We'd make the news and meet The Beatles just like that girl in New York who got Ringo's St. Christopher medal!"

"Judy! We're going home! And we're going home NOW!"

"I'll do it without you. I swear to God I will."

"Look," she said pointing to The Inn, "you'd need a ladder to get to the first set of balconies anyway. It's at least fifteen feet up to even get started."

I quickly looked around me in the parking lot, and there, as if by divine intervention, was a paint truck, complete with a twenty-foot ladder strapped to the side of it. I ran over to the truck faster than greased lightning and started frantically pulling at the ropes that secured the ladder.

"JUDY! Stop that! Are you nuts?!"

"Come on, Shell! Help me!"

"I can't…I just can't," she said and started to run away from me. "There they go!" I yelled after her, "my friend and her lack of continuity of purpose!"

"Teenage girls found their way to the rear of the hotel and like human flies began climbing from balcony to balcony in an attempt to see the group, or just one Beatle, or just to be able to say they saw the rooms."

—Robert F. Clifton, Atlantic City Police, August/
September 1983 issue of Beatlefan Magazine.
O☒cer Clifton was working security for the Beatles
at the Lafayette Motor Inn in August 1964.

CHAPTER FIFTY-THREE

I struggled with that twenty-foot ladder like a fisherman trying to land a 600-pound Marlin.

When I finally moved the ladder up against the wall of The Lafayette, I stopped, walked to the side of the building, walked around to the other side, and realized (gratefully) that absolutely no one at all was anywhere near me, *or* had a clue about what I was doing—except for Shelly, that is...wherever she was.

I positioned the ladder directly to the left of the first balcony and, I brought along the heavy rope that had tied the ladder to the truck just in case I needed to winch myself up a bit.

My plan was to make it there to Balcony Number One, and then climb the others diagonally or vertically, whatever worked, until I reached the top balcony of the building. Then, I would knock on the sliding glass door, and hopefully an understanding soul would answer it and show some kindness and compassion to a girl who was out on their private terrace after 3:00 AM, fifty feet above ground level.

I have always been an optimist.

I shook the ladder to make sure it was stable and then I moved my Ronette'd self upward toward my goal. My legs were a bit shaky, and I was scared, but, a combination of faith, hope, and stupidity had gotten me this far, so I wasn't about to stop now.

Within ten minutes I had not only made it to the first balcony, but I had also managed to finagle my way up two more floors.

As I was attempting to make it to the fourth floor, I heard a voice scream, "THERE'S A GIRL SCALING THE BACK WALL!"

By the time I hoisted my way up one more floor, I had an audience of at least a hundred girls supporting my effort, and six policemen not quite feeling the same.

Officer Stern called out to me, "I hope you realize you're in serious trouble young lady!"

I turned around and poofed my 'Ronette' hair. "Oh, I'm sorry officer, were you talking to me?"

The girls laughed and started to chant, "GO! GO! GO! GO!"

I grabbed the rope once again, prayed for God to send either a news crew or a Beatle my way and then swung over to another balcony.

"STOP RIGHT THERE, YOUNG LADY!"

By now the fire company had sent one of their trucks to The Inn and I was staring down at a huge crowd of "GO! GO!" Judy fans, a half a dozen cops, and the barrel of a very sturdy-looking fire hose.

"I SAID STOP!!!!" the officer yelled once again.

To discourage any further monkey-business (no pun intended) one of the firemen pointed the hose at me and gave me a good heavy spritz. That gave just enough time for some cops to enter the room where I was and then extract me from the balcony.

Two burly policemen opened the sliding door, lifted me straight up off of my feet, and right onto the red, orange, and yellow shag carpeting.

I was drenched.

I got a fast look at myself in the mirror as they moved me from the unoccupied room and out in the hall toward the elevator.

My beehive looked more like last year's bird's nest, and my cat-eyes once again looked as if I'd just gone fifteen rounds with Sonny Liston.

As I was being escorted down the hallway, I noticed the one officer's last name was, O'Brien.

"Hey, you don't have a brother who works in New York, do you? You know, up by the park?"

"Why? Have you been in trouble up there, too?"

"Me? No. Actually he kinda liked me."

"Well, then yes, I do. His name is Mike."

"Hey, when you talk to him, tell him Mary McGillicutty's niece said hello, okay?"

"You're Irish?"

"As I said to your brother, I'm as Irish as Paddy's Pig."

He gave my very sad physical state the once over and then said, "Actually, you look more like…"

"A poster girl for the Oktoberfest?"

He nodded. "Yeah, I can see that."

I rolled my eyes. *Here we go again!*

The minute the door to the elevator opened, there stood Officer Stern, and my nice chitchat with Rookie O'Brien was over.

"I'll take it from here."

Officer O'Brien and his partner started to walk down the hallway. He turned and said, "Take care, McGillicutty!"

The elevator door closed, and Stern looked at me, "McGillicutty?"

"It's a long story, Sir."

"I bet it is. And guess what?"

"What?"

"I don't wanna hear it."

We reached the lobby, and I was told to sit down on the leatherette sofa that was positioned in-between elevator one and the Coke machine.

I touched the top of my hair and it felt like a pile of hay glued onto my head, and my eye makeup was dripping down my face and onto my neck. I was cold, wet, and when I looked down, more good news: both of my nylons had ripped, and my knees were sticking completely through them. Now there was a sight: black sheer stockings and these two ugly white knees, banged up, dirty, and bruised, bulging right on out of them.

I'd seen better days for sure.

Officer Stern took one more look at me and went straight in for the kill. He had all of my personal information because of our reservation data, and he made it perfectly clear to me that he did.

"1120 Wakeling Street?"

"Yes."

"CUmberland 8-9809?"

"Yes. Are you gonna call my parents?"

"Now what do *you* think?"

"I..."

"You what?"

"Well, I...I wouldn't advise you calling my mother at this time of the night, because she..."

"Don't tell me what to do!" he snapped at me.

I took a deep breath and tried to hold back the tears.

He made a fast call on his walkie-talkie, and I heard him say, "Get a paddy wagon over here. NOW!"

Immediately, I spoke up. "Officer Stern? You're not arresting me, are you? I mean, on...on what charges?"

He pulled out a small, lined tablet and read, "Destruction of private property, theft, inciting a riot, four counts of resisting arrest, and solicitation."

"You know it really sounds bad when you put it that way."

"Don't be a wise-ass. You're in enough trouble."

I thought for a moment and then said, "Solicitation?!"

"You heard me."

"I wasn't selling anything! Listen, the last thing I ever sold was Girl Scout cookies back in 1955!"

He gave me a dirty look and then turned away from me.

Oh, brother...

I sat there and tried hard to think my way out of my latest predicament, but I just couldn't. The well was dry...and I was doomed.

I put my head full of Aqua Netted/Ronette'd hair in-between my soggy wet knees and prayed for divine intervention.

Dear God in heaven...please help me...whatever you can do to get me outta this mess, just do it! I'll never screw up again. Well, at least I'll try to never...

Just then, I heard the elevator door open, and I looked up to see who it was. There, not five feet away from me, stood George Harrison.

GEORGE HARRISON!

WHAT!?!

Yup. George Harrison!!!

...Grey suit, Chesterfield collar, and those beautiful black Beatle boots.

My hands shook, my heart fluttered, and once again I quickly dropped my head down in-between my knees.

Nowhere to run...nowhere to hide!

George paused for a moment and then walked over to the soda machine. I heard the dime clink, and then he walked right back in front of me. And when I say in front of me, I mean it. With my head bowed down in-between my knees, all I could see were his feet right up against mine.

I had to look up.

…There was that crooked smile.

Oh, my God! This man is so beautiful!

He handed me a white linen handkerchief that had the initials 'GH' sewn on it, in what appeared to be black silk.

"Here ya go," he smiled again.

I barely managed to squeak out a thank you. I reached for his handkerchief with five broken turquoise fingernails and, as lady-like as possible, I dabbed at my eyes and my neck. When I looked at his handkerchief once again, it was an absolute mess, nothing but black Egyptian eyeliner, and very little white left to be seen.

I held it out to him. "I'm…I'm awfully sorry."

He smiled that crooked smile once again. "Just keep it. Are you okay?"

"Well…"

George was standing so close to me that I could actually feel his sweet, warm breath upon my face. And, as if the most natural thing in the world to do, I found myself slowly breathing him in, thinking to myself…no…SCREAMING to myself—JUDY!!! MY GOD!!! YOU'VE GOT GEORGE HARRISON'S BREATH IN YOUR LUNGS!!!

Again, he repeated, "Are you okay?"

I exhaled v-e-r-y s-l-o-w-l-y. "Well, I…"

"Alright, sister," Officer Stern bellowed, "the wagon's on its way! And I'm *personally* calling your parents the minute we get you to the station!"

George immediately asked, "What's all this?"

"She's a troublemaker. Thanks to you and her bad taste in music."

I sniffled and said, "They're...they're charging me with destruction of private property, theft, inciting a riot, four counts of resisting arrest, and s-s-solicitation."

"Ya know," George said, "it really sounds bad when you put it that way."

I nodded in agreement. "That's what I said!"

"Solicitation?" George questioned me.

I shrugged my shoulders. "It was just Girl Scout cookies back in '55!"

Once again, Officer Stern stood right beside me. "Let's go, Little Miss Rabble-Rouser! You've seen the last of this place."

I immediately started to cry and cough and wheeze and cry and...

George handed me his bottle of Coca-Cola. "You could prob'ly use this."

I touched his hand as I reached for the bottle.

Oh, my God...I touched him! I touched him!!!

I sniffled back a very nervous and very shaky, "Thank you."

"Look," he said to Stern, "if she's in trouble because of what you think she did because of me or the group, then I'll take the heat for it."

Stern said nothing.

"What's the destruction of property thingy?"

"She bent one of those large ashtrays in the lobby."

"Bent an ashtray? And?"

"She stole a ladder off a paint truck in the parking lot."

"So where is it now?"

"My officers secured it back on the truck."

"Inciting a riot?"

Stern shook his head. "She was a hundred feet off the ground swingin' on a rope on her way to see you! You think that didn't cause a ruckus with your fans?"

George turned toward me. "Too many Tarzan films, ay?"

"I liked the monkey."

"And resisting arrest?" George asked Stern.

"Well, she wasn't exactly happy about us catching her," he said sarcastically.

"I wouldn't be either. …Solicitation?"

"That…that was a mistake. Officer O'Brien just cleared that one up for me. She was in the lobby when some ladies of the evening were visiting here. A case of wrong time and wrong place."

"Just let her go then. There's no reason to put her through all this."

My heart lightened and I took another swig of his soda.

George walked back over to me and said, "You won't be gettin' into any more trouble here, now will ya?"

"No."

"Promise?" His lip curled a bit.

"I promise."

Then he smiled at me again.

Stern knew he was beaten, and I heard him call for the wagon to go back to the station. "Alright, go on," Officer Stern said to me in a softer voice than usual, "Now get out…"

"I know. …and stay out."

I pushed my soggy wet self up off the sofa and then turned toward George. "Thank you… for everything."

"You're very welcome."

I watched as he pushed the elevator button.

"George?"

"Yah?"

"You…you want your soda back?" I held it out in his direction. My hand was trembling.

My hero shook his beautiful shaggy head. "I bought it for you."

"For me?"

He nodded and smiled.

He bought it for me?! Me?!! FOR ME?!!!!

I lovingly clutched the bottle to my chest. One ten-cent Coca-Cola and I couldn't have been happier if someone else had just dropped The Hope Diamond into my lap.

Then, suddenly, the elevator opened, and I followed George with my eyes as he moved into it. He held the door steady with his right hand, and, for just a moment, he stood there watching me.

I looked back at him, totally mesmerized, and vowed to hold that image of George in my mind so that it would last me for the rest of my life.

"You know," I said with tears in my eyes, "meeting you, I mean…well…" I looked down at myself and the mess that I was, and continued, "well, it was supposed to be, I mean…I'd always hoped for it to be such a…a beautiful moment and…"

"And it was," he smiled at me.

Then, as I had only seen him do on stage, in front of thousands and thousands of fans, he took a bow.

For me.

Only me.

Without another word spoken, the elevator door slowly closed…and my favorite Beatle, my newfound hero, my darling George…was gone.

CHAPTER FIFTY-FOUR

Officer Stern started barking at me again, but I didn't hear a word he said. I just floated on wings right out of the front entrance.

I had only flown about ten feet, when I heard Shelly calling out to me. "JUDY! JUDY! Oh, my God! I'm so sorry I left you, but I was sooooo scared and…"

Just then Officer O'Brien rode by in a squad car and stopped me.

"Hey, McGillicutty! I heard George Harrison saved you from a trip in the paddy wagon. Now there's one to put into the old diary, huh?"

I smiled at him. "You can say that again!"

I started to walk up North Carolina Avenue toward the beach. A new day was just about to break, and I wanted to see it front and center.

Shelly was practically jogging alongside of me, asking one rapid-fire question after the other: "George Harrison?! Jude! My God! George! You met George?! Looking like that?! And what?

He stopped you from going to jail? Where was he? How did it happen? What was it?! COME ON, TELL ME!!! TELL ME!!!!!!!"

Within minutes Shelly and I were sitting on a wooden bench watching the sunrise and I explained everything in perfect detail: my 'Zippy the Chimp' moves swinging from balcony to balcony, gettin' hosed down by the Atlantic City Fire Department, the two cops who caught me, Officer Stern, and…the elevator door that opened barely five feet away from me, containing one absolutely gorgeous George Harrison—straight to my rescue.

She laughed, "So, like he got off on the wrong floor or something?"

"I don't know."

"*You* are one lucky girl. Thank God for George. Your parents woulda hung you out to dry!"

"To say the least."

She laughed again, "And after *all* you went through to have your 'date' with a Beatle, and this is what ya got?! I mean, geez, whatta mess!"

I sighed and then took the very last sip of the soda that George had so graciously given to me.

"Jude?"

"Yeah?"

"Correct me if I'm wrong, but didn't you always say that when you finally met George it would be the most beautiful moment in your entire life?!"

Once again, I saw his handsome face before me, heard that perfect Liverpudlian accent…

"And it was," I smiled at Shelly…"It was."

AND IN THE END...

Judy attended nine Beatles concerts in total, from 1964 thru 1966—to include the famous Shea Stadium concert on August 15th, 1965.

Her loyalty to the Fab Four remains a constant to this very day, although a bit more subdued than in her younger years.

Scan the QR code to find other amazing adventures and more from www.ImagineAndWonder.com

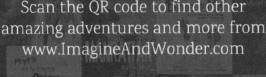

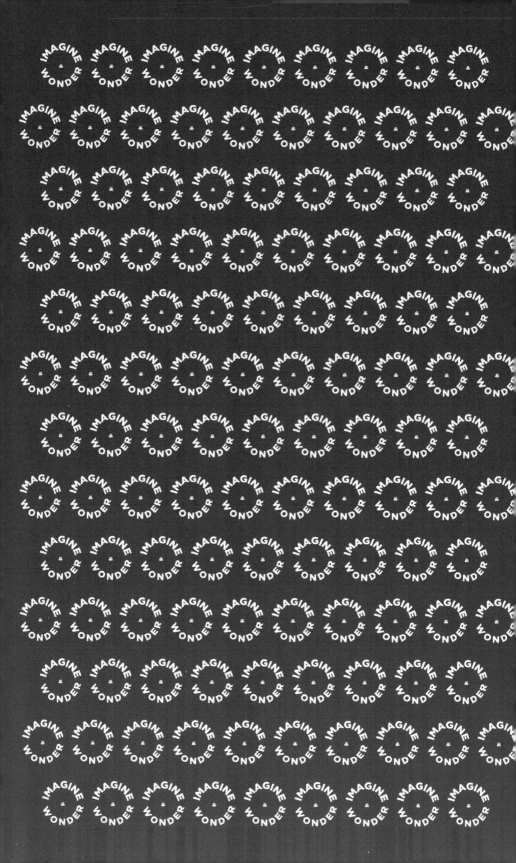